Death of the American Heart

A BLUEPRINT TO ENGAGE THE SILENT MAJORITY

Peter Hughes

ISBN: 1452890617
ISBN-13: 9781452890616

Library of Congress Control Number: 2010907640

Death of the American Heart

A BLUEPRINT TO ENGAGE
THE SILENT MAJORITY

We, the People, deserve a better, more effective government.

We, the People, deserve to see our elected officials conduct the people's business in an honest and forthright manner, unencumbered by the influence of special interest groups.

We, the People, deserve to see honest, responsible, and respectful debate by all elected officials.

We, the People, deserve honest business leaders and union officials.

We, the People, deserve better schools, teachers, and administrators.

We, the People, deserve to have our national traditions honored.

We, the People, deserve to have good health care at a reasonable price for all Americans.

We, the People, deserve cities and towns without high levels of crime, corruption, and crumbling infrastructures.

We, the People, deserve a better, more secure life for our families.

We, the People, deserve to see our children and their children have a brighter, more successful, and prosperous future, and not be burdened by the financial sins of our current government.

We, the People, deserve to live in peace and be strongly defended when threatened by outside forces of evil.

We, the People, deserve to be listened to and respected by our government officials regarding our opinions and ideas.

We, the People, deserve to be able to live our lives free of government constraints, regulations, laws, and controls that impinge upon our constitutional freedoms and don't make any sense.

We, the People, deserve better.

Acknowledgments

I dedicate this book to my lovely wife, Alicia, for her many years of loving me; my wonderful children, Peter John, Aimee, Patrick, Jonathan and my seven other grandchildren.

My thanks to Brooks Winchel, my daughter Aimee Lilly, and my wife Alicia, who provided me with early editing support and insight into how best to organize and structure certain chapters.

I want to acknowledge and thank my spiritual mentor and role model, the Blessed Mother. Her very caring presence has guided my thinking, actions, and behavior over the years. As with my wife, Alicia, she has been a positive force in my life.

I must thank my mother and father, Ann and Jack Hughes, who consistently stressed and reinforced throughout my childhood that one must live one's life guided by a core set of principles. One must not lie, cheat, steal, or hurt others. I hope that I am reflecting those guiding principles in the text and ideas contained in this book.

Finally, I must acknowledge, as painful as it is for me to do so, the Notre Dame nuns, who for eight long years literally pounded a strong set of values into my head, and the Augustine fathers, who honed and reinforced those values through a disciplined and structured high school education.

Table of Contents

Why This Book

I have written this book in the hope that it will stimulate your heart and soul, and inspire you to become an agent for transformational social change. I would like to believe that the pendulum will swing back toward our nation's founding principles, and that my children and grandchildren will not have to experience the pain, suffering, and hopelessness associated with an America with no sense of vision and purpose for building a great, self-sustaining, and values-driven society.

The writing of this book was not a research project. As I lay in a hospital bed during the month of October 2008, recovering from major surgery, I had the chance to watch a lot of the presidential campaign debates and rallies. I became increasingly frustrated by the negativity on the part of the politicians, news commentators, and Washington pundits. I also had been concerned about where our great nation was headed regarding its moral compass, educational system, manufacturing industry, and status in the world community. So for twenty-nine days, I started to organize my thoughts for this book. What you will find in these pages are my thoughts, feelings, emotions, knowledge, and experiences as an average American citizen. I consider myself to be a member of the silent majority who has reached a point of great frustration with the current state of affairs in the United States. I feel compelled to speak out regarding what I believe are the forces at play that are destroying our nation and way of life. These forces, if not addressed, will create dire negative consequences for the quality of life our children and grandchildren will experience as American citizens.

We are becoming Europeanized as we lose the many aspects of world leadership we have demonstrated in the past as a leading and prosperous nation. Whether it is our industrial manufacturing segments or our high-tech industries, we are losing our competitive position in the global marketplace. We are striving toward a state of mediocrity and socialized thinking and behaving. We need to, and we must, reinvent our society if we are to pass along the legacy of continued success, prosperity, and freedom to our children's children.

If I can stimulate the thought process of a few members of our country's silent majority to get involved and start to push for the changes I have outlined in this book, then my words will have meant something and I can go about the rest of my life dedicated to improving the lives of our citizens.

I will not be able to reach the far left, nor will I be able to reach the far right with my ideas. These groups have become entrenched in a polarizing, positional war and have lost sight of what is in the best interest of America. They are mentally and physically consumed with satisfying the needs of their special interest groups and achieving their myopically focused agenda. They have lost their ability to engage in constructive discourse and debate regarding the future direction of our country. Many of these pundits personally attack others who espouse a different view of the possibilities for our country. These two groups won't listen to the will of the silent majority because they are engaged in a win/lose battle, focusing on complete victory for their side at the expense of the real needs of our country.

I can, however, and hope to, touch the hearts and souls of the people who make up the center of the political thinking spectrum of our country, to engage in a quiet revolution of thoughts and ideas. This is the group that, with their votes, voices, and passion, can help to reinvent this great nation with values and principles that honor those Americans who gave so much to see that we would live free of tyranny and oppression…free to pursue our individual dreams and aspirations…free to strive to become what those inner passions are moving us toward…free to prosper and grow in a society built on a solid foundation of values…free to enjoy the fruits of our labor, unencumbered by excessive taxes and regulations…and free to enjoy life with our families and friends without too much governmental interference.

It is this silent majority that I hope to reach with my message of transformation, hope for our children's future, and commitment to regain our leadership, moral compass, and compassion as we lay our country's operating foundation for the next fifty years.

It is this collection of diverse citizens, this tapestry of wisdom and knowledge that I hope to encourage, with the words in this book, to become an energizing force and start to push back and demand reforms in our government, school systems, communities, and businesses.

Let me define what I mean when I use the term "silent majority." The silent majority consists of loyal, hardworking, peace-loving, law-abiding, and caring American citizens. There is no one dominant political party that makes up this silent majority. It consists of independents, Democrats, Republicans, socialists, libertarians, and others with diverse political ideologies. There is no dominant religious, ethnic, or social group. This powerful group of Americans is made up of those from all religions as well as atheists. It consists of all ethnic groups, along with people from all over the world who happen to be living and working in the United States. It is not identified by age or gender because men and women in all age brackets make up the fabric of this tapestry. Its members are, however, mothers and fathers, sons and daughters, schoolteachers and police officers, factory workers and doctors, university professors and retail employees, government workers and truck drivers. It is your neighbors, but most importantly, it is a group of wonderful and caring Americans who have had enough of the greed, selfishness, irresponsibility, and indecent behavior demonstrated on the part of our government officials, special interest groups, business and union leaders, and citizens. This book is intended for people who believe that, while the system is broken now, it can be fixed with forward-thinking solutions, such as the ones offered in this book.

Chapter 1

An Introduction

All throughout recorded history, there has always been a dominant civilization: from the ancient Greeks, Egyptians, Romans, Byzantines, Ottomans, Japanese, Mayans, and the dynasties of China, to, more recently, the French, Spanish, British, Portuguese, German, Russian, and American civilizations. These were the civilizations that advanced technology, math, science, medicine, agriculture, and commerce. Where are some of these civilizations today? Why have some not survived, endured, and sustained their greatness? Why are some that have survived in a state of mediocrity? What happened to these great societies, and what is currently happening to America?

Simply stated, some of the civilizations lost their visionary leadership and moral compass. Their political figures or ruling elite became corrupted by power. They lost their visions of greatness; they lost touch with their average citizens. They enslaved, brutalized, manipulated, punished, starved, and murdered the very people that made their societies great. They used religion and superstition as weapons of fear and intimidation. They became overzealous with power and prestige. They felt they were above the law of humanity. They tortured, maimed, and murdered anyone who challenged their authority, decisions, or actions. They became evil, unsympathetic, uncaring, immoral, and insensitive to the struggles of their people. Greed and avarice motivated their leaders, while power corrupted their thinking.

While these leaders indulged in the finest of food and wine, dressed in rich clothing, and disassociated themselves from the common citizens, the masses yearned for leadership and a better life. The average person wished for peace and prosperity, but the leaders wanted conquests, territory, riches from other civilizations, greater wealth, and more power. As a result, some of these great civilizations imploded, and others were conquered by civilizations that used new weapons and tactics as they invaded and destroyed the defending armies.

The United States has not learned well from history. We are following in the path of the great civilizations of the past that imploded, collapsed, or were conquered. This book will profile why we, as a country, are self-destructing, and why we have already transitioned from a great society to a good society, on our way to becoming an average society.

We are approaching a time in the near future when we might hear others say some of the following comments:

- There is nothing special about the United States.
- It does not lead the world in science and technology development, medicine, food production, or manufacturing.
- Its citizens are complacent, undereducated, overweight, out of shape, and looking for a handout.
- Its productivity is not very impressive.
- It is not a very caring, compassionate, creative, or resilient group of people.

All the stories I have heard about the "ugly American" seem to be true. This description is not how we should ever allow our nation to be perceived, but if we sit back and do nothing, if we allow the cancer that is devouring our country's soul to continue to ravage our nation, we will in fact become the world's greatest failure. Our civilization's decline will have been so great that what happened and why it happened will be studied a thousand generations from now.

The United States and its people have done more good on this earth for the poor and impoverished people of the world than all the other great civilizations combined. The sad fact is that when we are gone, the world will suffer a great loss. We cannot allow this to happen on our watch. We owe it to our children and their children to stop the madness that is happening in our society.

As a society, we have lost our moral compass. We have fractured the family, we have bullied the world, we have focused on wealth and instant gratification, and we have discarded the values and guiding principles of our founding fathers and the millions of people who sacrificed their lives so we could live free and prosper. We have left God behind and stripped our society of any religious symbols, traditions, or beliefs that once acted as the backbone of our nation. We can, with the right leadership, reverse the negative trend, but I do not think we have the stomach or the fortitude to make the tough decisions that are required to stem the tide of failure, complacency, and moral decay. I hope I am wrong.

As you will read in the following chapters, I identify a convergence of forces that is feeding the cancer that is killing our country. One day, we will cease to exist as a superpower, and we will eventually become subordinate to China. Our educational system is broken. Our political system is dysfunctional. Our spirit as a proud people has been dampened by corruption. Our manufacturing capacity, which used to be the best in the world, barely exists. Our great cities are in decay. Crime and corruption flourish in every part of society. Our religious organizations are crippled by scandal and dwindling membership. Our citizens are overweight, unfit, and self-absorbed. Our children are undereducated and lack the moral training that those before them had and manifested throughout their lives. We are obsessed with video games and pornography. Television shows portray the family as a dysfunctional unit and fathers as incompetent fools and idiots. Violence and immorality are everywhere, and God is being purged from our society.

In addition, we are losing our traditions. We no longer say "Christmas"; we say, "It's the holiday season." We no longer say "Christmas tree"; we say "holiday tree." Where did Saint Valentine's Day go? What happened to old Saint Nick? Even the Easter Bunny has been denied its rightful place in society. The Easter Bunny has been renamed the "spring bunny." Just recently, a federal judge in district court ruled that our National Day of Prayer that is held in May is unconstitutional. This will most likely go to the Supreme Court for a ruling, but it represents a microcosm of what is happening throughout our country. From the Ten Commandments to our Pledge of Allegiance, from a nativity scene

at Christmas to "In God We Trust" on our money, these signs and symbols are being challenged by people who object to any reference to
God. We will, however, embrace vulgarity, nudity, and sexually explicit
advertising, but will object to anything religious or righteous. Recently Provincetown, Massachusetts, created a school policy that autho-
rized the distribution of condoms to children five years old and up.
The Provincetown school system made it a policy that a five-year-old
child could receive a condom if he or she asked for one. The Provincetown school administration is concerned with making sure condoms
are available to elementary school children, but at what cost? Is this
policy really necessary? Should we not be more concerned with why
our math and science standings in the world community are slipping
further in the rankings against those nations we will compete with in
the global marketplace?

We are becoming a pathetic society, degrading into a second-
class country. We complain about everything that does not go our
way. We do not accept responsibility for our actions and decisions. Our
children have terrible role models shaping their behavior and moral
character. Some TV, film, and entertainment icons, as well as sports
stars, behave in immoral ways and corrupt the young and innocent
minds of our children with sex, violence, drugs, alcohol, and divorce
as what they espouse through their behavior as "success." In the rap
music our children listen to as their source of musical entertainment, it
seems like it is okay, even very cool, to use profanity, degrade women,
and exhort the virtues of violence.

In a subsequent chapter, I will talk about the need for a strong
third party in the United States because our current political system is
dysfunctional and corrupted by power and personal greed. I thought
when we elected officials to represent us in Washington, they would
be acting in the best interest of the state they represent first, and the
country they serve second. I did not expect our elected officials to
work for special interest groups or to support their political party at
the expense of the state and the people they represent just because
they are fencing with the president or the other party. Where has the
character of our politicians gone? There is nothing but a river of blame.
Most of our elected officials lack a sense of personal accountability
and integrity.

A good example can be seen in the comments regarding the failings of Fannie May, Freddie Mack, AIG, and the financial system. In these comments, there is a level of dishonesty and finger-pointing, not to mention the greed that drove many politicians and corporate managers to defraud the public that entrusted them to do what is right. Those two groups did not care about the average American citizen. The only things they cared about were profiting from a corrupt system and gorging themselves on a banquet of ill-gotten gains and graft.

A darkness and emptiness have fallen upon our great nation. We have vacant buildings in a state of decay that once stood tall and represented our industrial manufacturing leadership and innovation. They now languish in the quiet hours of their death. Our citizens, who used to be caring, loving, and supporting of neighbors and others in need, now have empty hearts. They are filled with selfishness and a preoccupation with "what's in it for me?" We have empty minds. Minds that used to be filled with wisdom and worldly knowledge are now filled with selfish thoughts and mindless social clutter. We have empty souls. Souls that were filled with a sense of purpose and meaning are now aimlessly wandering in a sea of greed, hopelessness, and despair. The light of passion has been replaced with the darkness of self-absorption and evil.

If the tone of my comments seems dark or negative, it is because I am deeply concerned for the future of my grandchildren and their children. If we, as a united country, do not change our ways, our children and their children will suffer immense pain and anguish as our country rots from within and our special way of life slips into an abyss of hopelessness and despair. We cannot allow this to happen. We must turn the tide before it is too late. We owe it to our children and all those who come after us. We cannot allow them to become enslaved in a pitiful society and new world order where the United States is no longer a leading nation but a nation of self-absorbed followers.

It was very difficult for me to write this book because I have been an optimist all my life and have operated with the glass always being half full. I have believed that in every breakdown, there is the possibility of a breakthrough. But as the years pass, I continue to see our society slip deeper into one that honors greed over God, that is more concerned about blaming others than sitting down and solving problems, that permits evil to corrupt our children while condemning those who try to right the wrongs, that allows transgressions against the good people of our country while protecting the rights of the perverted, where it is more important to be politically correct than to honor traditional values. These are the conditions that stoked my heart of hearts with the passion to say we must stop the insanity, because if we don't, my children's children will suffer immensely.

I have written this book so that you might find it in your heart to get involved, to demand reform, to become an agent for positive cultural change. I define you, the reader, as any American citizen who cares enough for the welfare of their children, and their children, to stand up and get involved and push for reforms that will get our nation and various social systems back on a course that is in alignment with our founding principles. This book is a blueprint for people who, because of their values and passion, say, "Enough is enough; we have gone too far and we need to reinvent our spirit as a great nation." I hope the readers of this book will, with their voices, votes, and passion, stand up against the corruption of our country's soul and commit to make a positive difference.

Chapter 2

Our Beginning Values

The Initial Power and Influence of the Pilgrims, Patriots, and Pioneers

Values, work ethic, personal integrity, and responsibility. The lessons from the Great Depression. Our values of the past.

Early in our development, we were blessed by the power, influence, and legacy of what I call the three P's of our great nation. The three P's refer to the values and spirit of America that was forged in blood, sweat, and tears by the pilgrims, patriots, and pioneers. These early values and the American spirit acted as the foundational building blocks as our nation took root and flourished.

These values and the spirit of America became the beacon of hope for millions of immigrants who had a vision of creating something very special in their lives and the lives of their children. The melting pot became the innovative engine of the world. To be realistic in my assessment, if one looks through the prism of history to any century of our nation's development, there are events and behaviors that were wrong, but over time were righted as best as possible. The way we cheated and disrespected the Native American tribes. The stain of slavery and how it shamed our country's soul. The sinfulness of racial discrimination, which still exists in various but declining forms today. How we welcomed and treated certain immigrant populations that came to this great land to pursue their dreams and give their families hope for a better future. Whether they were Chinese, Italian, Polish, or Irish, if they were not part of the white Anglo-Saxon Protestant lineage, they were condemned to slum living and menial jobs. And, of course, let us not forget women, who still to this day struggle for equality.

However, as I alluded to above, we as a country have acknowledged these transgressions against our fellow Americans, and as slow and painful as it seemed sometimes, we have tried our best to right these wrongs.

Have we finished addressing these issues? The answer is no, not all of them. We still have a lot of work to do, but we are making progress and have always been guided by the hand of justice. Sometimes, however, it has taken someone to stir the soul of the melting pot to bring a new vision and force of passion to change a situation or set of conditions that are not compatible with our espoused values as a nation. So, as your read the following section please keep in mind the historical context of the different developmental periods of our nation.

Let's reacquaint ourselves with how it all started and why we are at a decisive crossroads as a country, with one fork leading to second-rate status and another fork leading to sustained greatness as a leader of the free world.

It all began on the shores of England. On a cold and foggy day, a group of people who wanted a better life and the ability to freely practice their religion set sail with a vision of building something special and lasting, a new life, a calling to the greatness that their God had shared with them. They wanted a life that they could control, as well as an environment that would allow them to raise their children in accordance with their beliefs and teachings. This was all that they wanted: simple freedom. Freedom to do what they thought was right for themselves and their families.

For this freedom, they gave up life in a civilized world for life in a wild and dangerous new world. They gave up the comforts of England for the hardships of the New England forest and winters. They gave up most of their possessions for the right to make the journey across a hostile and unforgiving ocean and build everything from scratch. They gave up the warmth, comfort, and security of their homes for a journey that would take months in below-deck quarters filled with dampness, darkness, and the stench of sickness and disease—and discomfort and despair became their traveling companions. Some gave up their health and eventually their lives for this powerful vision of freedom. Still, they gave up these things because the power of their magnetic north vision dictated that the sacrifice would be worth it in the new world.

Based on my study of early American history, visits to Plymouth and Boston, Massachusetts, and a curiosity and interest I had developed for King Phillip and the King Phillip Wars, I started to piece together what I believed were the core fundamental values of these remarkable individuals and early Americans.

What I was able to distill as the core foundational values that made up the tapestry of desire and behavior of this special group of Americans is listed below:

- Self-sacrifice for the betterment of others
- Trust in God
- Belief in their abilities
- Respect for others
- Commitment to their word
- Honor
- Integrity
- Strong work ethic
- Vision
- Fortitude
- Ingenuity
- Resourcefulness
- Responsibility
- Accountability
- Commitment to family, friends, neighbors, and strangers
- Loyalty
- Honesty
- Sharing with others
- Overcoming adversity
- Compassion
- Empathy
- Taking risks

These core values shaped the attitudes and behavior of generations of pilgrims. They were the basis for our early laws, commerce, education, and religion. Some call them the "Puritan ethic." Others refer to them as our founding principles. Many of these core values would later become the basis for the Constitution of the United States. This document still acts as the beacon of light that guides our nation through periods of discontent and through the troubled waters of today.

Of course, the early settlers were not without faults. They destroyed many great and proud Indian civilizations. They had faults, but those faults need to be looked at and analyzed in the context of the historical period in which they occurred, and not through the lens of today's modern societal behavior norms and responsibilities. Did they go to excess with certain values and beliefs? The answer is a resounding yes. Again, those excesses need to be viewed in the context of the historical time in which they occurred.

Overall, we can describe the early pilgrims as very hardworking, family-oriented individuals who labored day and night just to survive and keep their vision of freedom alive. They first built homes and then a created community. The community gave way to cities, and finally the cities gave way to a great nation.

Sweat, blood, and sacrifice became the mortar that would hold the bricks of this new nation together. Sickness and death did not dissuade them from their vision to create a new nation where people were free to pray and practice their religion. Their journey was hard and painful. Their road was covered with the tears of many who lost loved ones while building the foundation of this great nation. They never gave up. They never wavered from their vision. They overcame impossible odds and sacrificed greatly so that their children would have a better life. We should all take a moment to try to understand what incredible feats they accomplished and the pain they endured to build a solid base for a great nation to come.

Next came the patriots. These were men and women who in some cases sacrificed not only their wealth and health but everything they had, including their sons and daughters, to keep the dream alive:

a dream of a nation free of tyranny, a nation of men and women free to make decisions and choices about their futures, lives, religion, and government, and free to live and prosper without undue government interference or taxation. They were men and women free to pursue their dreams and visions, free to be free. It took a revolution to ensure these freedoms would be available for generations to come, and many of these patriots shed their blood and gave their lives so we Americans could enjoy these liberties today.

Once again, values surfaced that would guide and influence, in extraordinary ways, the individual behavior of these creators of our nation's independence. Much has been written about those incredible times and about the men and women who sacrificed so much so that we could live our lives in a free and prosperous nation. We owe these patriots a great debt for the nation they formed and the wonderful life most Americans live today. The positive energy force these great Americans created was fueled by the values and beliefs that still reso-nate today in most of our communities, which include: independence, freedom, opportunity, sharing, giving, caring, self-sacrifice, love of country, and love for our fellow Americans.

These values can be witnessed today on the streets of Washington, D.C., and throughout all American cities and towns as the Tea Party debates take place. Whether or not you agree with the current Tea Party debates, what is clear and true is that in many other countries of this world, you would not be able to voice your opposition to your government's decisions and directions without dire consequences—in some cases, death. It is because of the shared values that the patriots included as the foundational building blocks of our Constitution and Bill of Rights that our citizens can express themselves without fear of reprisal, imprisonment, or other dreadful consequences.

Finally, the pioneers hardened the silos of values and beliefs that were the underpinnings of this great country. The lure of free land— land so fertile and rich that it was irresistible to farmers and their fami-lies living on the East Coast—the opportunity to own the fruits of their labor, to leave the industrial mills to pursue the American dream, and the chance to build new farms and communities motivated whole groups of neighbors to pull up stakes and move westward in pursuit of a new life for their families. Finally, for some, it was the adventure of new experiences and the pursuit of their ultimate dreams and passions that drove them. The early pioneers did not travel a path that was well-worn by those before them. They created the path, carving it with their blood, sweat, and tears as they went. They could see the joys and opportunities just over the next hill.

Think of the challenge of packing every one of your life's possessions, including your farm animals, into a tiny wooden wagon pulled by horses or oxen and traveling thousands of miles to establish a new life. It was a mission that was almost impossible. Their dreams and vision helped them cross mountain ranges, wild rivers, hostile territory, and drought in desert areas, freezing in winter and sweating in summer. These Americans did not have electricity, cell phones, microwave ovens, TVs, air-conditioning, bottled water, prepackaged food, or any of the comforts you and I are used to enjoying. The only things they had were fortitude, desire, inner motivation, passion, and a great sense of purpose—a burning desire to improve their lot in life for themselves and their children.

You can now start to get a feel for the special traits these extraordinary groups of American citizens embodied. The sacrifices we are asked to make today pale in comparison to the obstacles these individuals overcame, the feats they achieved, and the accomplishments they made in solidifying our nation's future success. We should be grateful to all those who have gone before us to forge a great nation with their desire and vision of something wonderful for future generations. How many of us would be willing to sacrifice everything we own, to endure great hardships, so America could live on and prosper for those yet to stand on the special soil of this, the greatest place on earth? Let's make sure we honor their sacrifices as we go about the business of sustaining our success as a nation.

Chapter 3

Overview of the Current State of the United States

Current Trends

There are some very disturbing trends in our country that point to its collapse. As a society, we are more concerned with ourselves, our wealth, and our comfort, and less concerned with the less fortunate. We are preoccupied with material things and less occupied with spiritual things. Our borders are broken, our educational system lags behind that of much of the developed world, our political system is corrupted with self-centered, greedy, and, in many cases, unethical politicians who think only of themselves and the special interest groups they claim they don't represent. Our infrastructure is collapsing around us in terms of roads, bridges, and transportation systems. Our trains are a far cry from those of Japan and Europe. Our highways are overcrowded, dirty, and in need of repair. A typical business day commute in many of our major cities turns out to be an extremely frustrating experience. What normally should take thirty minutes to get to your workplace ends up taking sixty and sometimes ninety minutes. Once you arrive at your destination, then the challenge becomes finding a reasonably priced parking space.

Another concerning current trend is the lack of a superior level of customer service, and the pervasive disrespectful attitude on the part of many organizations to which you and I are just a number. Simply stated, the notion of customer service is nonexistent in many of the transactions we have today when dealing with the companies, institutions, and government organizations necessary to get through life's challenges. As a customer, you are treated with disrespect—if you are lucky. In most cases, you are ignored. It is very difficult to find a human being to help you with your problems or at least answer your questions. You are forced to deal with a menu of options by pressing a series of buttons on your phone that, quite often, takes you somewhere you did not want to go or to someone who will transfer you to someone else, where you might have to deal with another series of numeric, menu-driven options. In addition, it is not uncommon to sit in an airport for hours waiting for your plane to leave, while you experience delay after delay with no communication from the airline personnel regarding what is happening.

I will touch on a few additional current trends that are having an impact on the slow decline of our society. The cost of medical coverage keeps going up, which is reflected in your co-pay assessment. At the same time, as a country we are about to embark on a major health-care reform process that has many people concerned about the impact on the quality of care, the access to quality care, and the cost to support the uninsured. Energy costs keep climbing without any explanation, yet we do not have a definite strategy to become energy-independent. People don't take the time to be civil to each other or to care about their neighbors. It's a selfish state of mind. There is a large percentage of our population looking for a free lunch.

- They are trying to get as much money and services from the government as they can, with no regard to whether or not they need them.
- They are the human pigs of our society or the locusts of the twenty-first century.
- They are the "entitled" trying to beat the system, claiming we owe them a living and they do not have to contribute anything in return.
- They gorge themselves at the trough that the government provides.
- In many cases, they do not pay taxes or don't pay their fair share.
- They demand but are not tolerant.
- They take but will not give.
- They consume but will not help grow.
- They are self-absorbed and will not share.
- They demand respect but will not respect others.
- They do not tolerate criticism but will criticize others.

- God is dead in the eyes of many, and the power of the dollar rules.
- Spirituality has been replaced by sexuality.
- Care for others has been replaced by insensitivity.

In addition, as a nation we have become insensitive to other cultures and political systems. We manifest the arrogance that everyone on the planet should act like we do, think like we do, and embrace the principles we embrace. The problem is, the world does not operate that way.

In this great nation, we have people dying because they cannot get adequate medical coverage. We have children going to bed hungry because they have no food. We have parents that can't parent. We have fathers and mothers blinded by drugs and alcohol at the expense of their family's well-being. We have children giving birth to babies, perpetuating the cycle of poverty and despair. We watch as some weekly television shows parade loser after loser on stage to discuss their personal problems, and we accept this level of degenerate behavior as part and parcel of our society. This is disgraceful.

At the same time, there is a major assault taking place on the middle class. Its members have been downsized from their jobs or asked to do more with less pay while executives get richer through outsourcing work to cheap labor markets. They have been overtaxed and underrepresented by their government. They have been cheated and abused by the health-care system, and denied access to certain programs and benefits because of their savings or income. They continue to be exploited by the credit card companies, banks, and government officials that are supposed to have their best interests at heart.

But there is hope. We can and will address these social issues and fix them. Currently, there are many good American citizens, religious organizations, and nonprofit groups trying to meet these social challenges and they are making some progress. However, they are underfunded and under-resourced, and in many cases because of the current economic situation in our country their funding is being reduced. As a nation, we must re-prioritize our strategic goals and muster the necessary resources to forcefully take on and correct these social issues.

I will make recommendations that are more specific in later chapters of this book.

Globalization

Free trade, globalization, and offshore outsourcing are very interesting subjects that have caused the very industrial heart of our nation to enter a state of atrophy and decline. Our government, especially under the Clinton and Bush administrations, entered into trade agreements without thoroughly researching the long-term impact on our industrial base, middle class, global competitiveness, or military security. These trade agreements have fueled the engine of outsourcing our jobs, plants, and manufacturing capabilities in the quest for the holy grail of cheap labor sources to build our products so we can make more profit for the shareholders. We have mortgaged our children's future so people can buy cheap goods at Wal-Mart-type warehouse stores.

As a result of globalization, we have educated the world's labor force about how to produce our products and provide our services. Consequently, foreign entities have developed their own capabilities and, in some cases, stolen our proprietary manufacturing secrets outright. While they pay their workers a few dollars a day and rarely provide benefits, we have become, almost overnight, unable to compete.

So we have acquiesced and given up our manufacturing industry to third-world countries. We have moved from a dominant manufacturing-driven economic base to a service sector-driven economic base. Service-based jobs are not the same as the skilled and semi-skilled jobs available in the manufacturing sector, as I will highlight later in this chapter. Also, it is the middle class and certain minority groups that are losing good career opportunities as jobs move offshore. As reported by *Industrial Week*'s staff members on December 3, 2009, the Alliance for American Manufacturing points out that manufacturing has lost five million jobs and fifty-one thousand plants in the past ten years. Many of these jobs have gone to China, Mexico, and other third-world countries where labor is cheap. Chris Isidore, a senior writer for CNNMoney.com, stated the recession killed off 7.9 million jobs. He goes on to say: "It's likely that many will never come back." When one looks at the surface, this is not a bad situation to be in, because our economy (GDP) is still growing yet the price of goods sold is dropping. It is a windfall for the lower-middle class because its members now can afford to buy merchandise that was previously priced out of their range.

However, this situation does come with a heavy long-term cost to our society, and what is troubling is that nobody is talking about this situation today with any consistency, except Lou Dobbs of CNN, and he no longer has a voice at that network during the evening news cycles. The following is a profile of the long-term negative side effects of our globalization policies.

- **Job Loss**

This, of course, is the most obvious negative side effect. I would wager that most Americans know of some family member, neighbor, or work colleague that has been downsized as a result of jobs being sent offshore. What's unfair is that corporate managers and senior executives still get their outrageous salaries, bonuses, and stock options because they have been able to keep the share price high. However, the cost in human misery of the American workers and suffering as a result of employees losing their jobs to people in China or India is not only unfair and immoral, it is un-American. Employees have lost their self-esteem and their homes. Their family members have often suffered the humiliation of not having an income, and many of those employees have reentered the workforce at much lower levels of pay and job responsibility. A significant number of those who have lost their jobs are now working in the service sector. However, as you will see, jobs at Wal-Mart, Home Depot, Lowe's, Target, etc., are not the same types of jobs or career opportunities that one would enjoy in the manufacturing sector.

- **Loss of Skilled and Semi-Skilled Career Opportunities**

As I mentioned above, the jobs in the service sector are not the same from a career opportunity point of view as the jobs in the manufacturing sector. There are a large number of high school students who, because of various circumstances, do not go on to pursue a college degree. When we had a strong manufacturing sector in this country, those young men and women could enter it and find enormous career opportunities. However, those opportunities are gone forever.

There was also a large amount of our population that was already working in the manufacturing sector. Here is a partial list of careers that are now dwindling for these individuals: machine operators, lathe operators, machinists, millers, grinders, tool and die makers, welders, painters, millwrights, manufacturing technicians, quality inspectors, lab technicians, planners, purchasing agents, engineers, electricians, instrumentation technicians, pipe fitters, warehousing support, material handling, packaging, facilities support, maintenance mechanics, truck drivers, forklift drivers, information technologists, lead operators, supervisors, and a variety of administrative functions.

These jobs are gone, and at least for the foreseeable future they are not coming back. This does not include the professional, management, and technical engineering positions that were required to support all of these skilled and semi-skilled disciplines. Jobs in sales, marketing, research and development, process engineering, quality control, finance, supply chain, human resources, and operations have disappeared as well, thereby displacing many in these professions with career-ending terminations. It is difficult to find a well-paying job of equal status and responsibility in this economy. It is very difficult if you are over forty, extremely difficult if you are over fifty, and next to impossible if you are over sixty and have been downsized from your job.

The following is the headline of an article written by Rex Nutting of *Market Watch* dated April 3, 2009; it might help to substantiate my points about job loss.

ECONOMIC REPORT

April 3, 2009

5.1 million jobs lost in this recession so far

Payrolls fall 663,000 in March while unemployment rate jumps to 8.5%

By Rex Nutting, MarketWatch

WASHINGTON (MarketWatch) - American workers were hammered again in March with large job losses, pushing the total number of jobs lost since the recession began to 5.1 million, the Labor Department reported Friday. U.S. nonfarm payrolls fell by 663,000 in March, close to expectations, while the unemployment rate jumped to a 26-year high 8.5% from 8.1%, as expected.

"This recession is far from over," wrote David Rosenberg and Sheryl King, economists for Bank of America's Merrill Lynch.

"There is nothing in this report that points to economic recovery," said economists at RDQ Economics. Details of the report confirm that the U.S. economy likely contracted violently again in the first quarter. Economists believe gross domestic product likely fell at a 5.5% annual pace after a 6.3% decline in the last three months of 2008.

This report is over a year old and things have gotten a lot worse. Unemployment is higher and good middle class jobs are still being sent offshore to cheap labor producing markets.

One of the contributing factors that has created a certain amount of job loss is our work ethic which is declining and driven by greed. Many people want to maximize their income while contributing the least amount of work. People are looking for a handout as opposed to working hard and sacrificing. They want it now—or should I say, the major thought process that appears to be the prevalent attitude of a good number of people in today's workforce is: what's in it for me?

Auto workers for example make significantly more than their counterparts in Japan and Korea, if you compare salary and their total benefit package including healthcare and retirement. Their union officials fight very hard to keep the existing wage, benefit and work rule structures in place. This situation makes us less competitive in the global marketplace and his contributed to a significant decline in market share over the last thirty years. If a U.S. auto worker happens to get laid off during a slack period, they still get a large percentage of their salary during that time. All of this as the U.S. auto industry crumbles financially and declines in market share. Furthermore, hefty bonuses and stock options are given to the executives of these companies while they enjoy the perks of corporate jets and executive dining rooms. This all happens while we are giving away our market to China, Japan, and Korea.

We lack a unifying vision for our country. We cannot compete effectively in the global marketplace because we lack the leadership in government to establish policies that will protect our core manufacturing industry.

We, as a country, have a quarter-to-quarter strategic focus, whereas Japan has a much longer strategic focus, and China's is even longer. We are graduating ten times more lawyers than we are engineers and scientists. We turn around and sue McDonald's because we are getting obese eating Big Macs and fried food. We blame everyone except ourselves for our problems.

We are a sick civilization and are getting sicker.

This is a short profile of the current state of the United States as I see it. However, in subsequent chapters I will expand on many of the negative societal conditions mentioned above.

Chapter 4

Our Moral Compass—Our Morality

As I mentioned previously, I believe we are in a rapid state of moral decline. This decline is manifested in the immoral content of television shows, movies, print media, the Internet, and the attitude toward any type of religious display.

The trends that are acting as forces of change within the United States are for the most part negative, from the television shows we watch that portray the family unit as dysfunctional, the father figure as incompetent, and the mother figure as starving for love and affection, to the news shows that deliver to us a vortex of negative statements, images, and a lack of socially mature and polite discourse. These negative trends influence the thinking of our citizens, creating unfit role models that act to shape the thinking and behavior of our youngest and, in many cases, most naïve population.

As a country, we are imploding. The economy is crumbling, unemployment is very high, and the smart Wall Street leaders and investment firms have raped and pillaged our national treasure.

Family values as modeled by our forefathers have been assaulted by the politically correct diversity movement, where same-sex marriage is replacing the time-honored tradition of a man and a woman bonding together in a love sealed by vows of loyalty, trust, and commitment. I support civil unions, and I can understand and support alternative lifestyles, but I hold the sanctity of traditional marriage above the alternative forms. Whether you are heterosexual or homosexual, it comes down to the integrity of your personal behavior and your modeling of appropriate values. Being married and cheating on your spouse or being in a relationship and cheating on your partner are a breach of trust and represent a disrespectful act toward the person you claim to love. If you cheat on your loved ones, you will cheat in other aspects of your life. I will address this issue in greater detail later in this book.

God is being expelled and defamed wherever He has watched over us or has been a sign and symbol of our cultural heritage—in schools, in public places, during holidays, in our Pledge of Allegiance, and on our money.

A large percentage of our citizens are overweight, under-educated, unfit, and lack a sense of personal responsibility for their behavior.

As I have stated and will clarify in the following chapters of this book, our government is bloated and dysfunctional, our educational system is failing our children, our financial systems have crashed, our infrastructure is crumbling, our manufacturing industry has been banished to China, and our image in the world is that of a bully.

Our morality is at an all-time low, with behavioral norms that reinforce the philosophy of "do your own thing and say what you want to say, even though it may be very offensive to others." Sexually explicit content and behavior is everywhere you look. It is in magazines, on television, on billboard advertisements, and demonstrated in the inappropriate behavior of men and women in key areas of responsibility or influence throughout our country.

The Internet is filled with filth, from child pornography to the most disgusting sexually explicit pictures. This type of deviance is a cancer that has destroyed civilizations in the past, and it has radically damaged our moral compass.

You may not like it, but there are great forces at work in our country, destroying our morality and causing the decline of the family, as well as weakening the core values that centered the family in the past. Values like respect, hard work, love, tolerance, and compassion are under attack.

The divorce rate is very high. The value to love and cherish until death do us part does not seem to carry the same level of influence in our lives. Extramarital affairs by both men and women seem to be flourishing as respect for each other dwindles and the flame of commitment dies. Many people think there is nothing wrong with flirting with the opposite sex, which may be true, but how far does that thinking extend? Is it fair to say, "I did not have sex with that woman," when in fact there was inappropriate touching of certain body parts? What about the most recent sex scandals that you have read about in the news or seen on the cable networks concerning Tiger Woods, Jesse James, and John Edwards? Where was their commitment to their wives?

How about the recent sex scandals involving two sitting governors? They are the chief executive officers for their respective states and each demonstrated a major breach of personal integrity. Character does, in fact, matter. It matters in business, it matters in sports, and it matters in entertainment. It matters in everyday life and in everything you do. However, some Americans think it is no big deal to lie and cheat on your spouse. Tiger did not ask to be a role model, nor did Jesse James, John Edwards, or the two state governors. But like it or not, when you are in the public eye and people look to you for leadership or as a role model to emulate, you have a responsibility to conduct your life with a high level of personal integrity. As I stated previously, if you lie and cheat on your spouse, there is a pretty good chance you will lie and cheat in other areas of your life. Who really suffers? Your spouse and children, first and foremost, but you will also deeply hurt many other people. **Character does matter** in your life's journey.

Greed

A classic current example of our moral decline as a country is what has happened during the recent financial crisis. Greed is so pervasive and such a powerful force in our society that it is destroying the very fabric of our existence as a world power. During our darkest days, when our economy was crashing to new lows, when men and women were losing their jobs by the millions and families were losing their homes, what happened in our financial institutions? Their executives assaulted the American citizens! They gorged at the taxpayers' dinner table and paid themselves billions of dollars in bonuses. At the same time, their lack of leadership caused their companies' performance to decline, and in some cases they even bankrupted their institutions. These are the institutions that the average American citizens trusted with their retirement money and their future financial security. The higher-ups in these organizations turned around and poked a stick in the eye of the American people with their greed for personal gain and their arrogance in spending the taxpayers' money on bonuses, lavish homes, trips to exotic places, elegant office improvements, and a work lifestyle that few of us will ever experience.

The American people suffered while these executives enjoyed their multiple mansions, yachts, and expensive standard of living. I believe in the scales of justice, and I would like to see many of these individuals go to jail. They have inflicted such an enormous amount of pain and suffering on the American people that they need to be held accountable. While they were laying people off and families were losing their life savings, these executives enjoyed a rich and extremely rewarding life with bonuses they received that should have gone into customers' 401(k) retirement accounts. However, because of questionable investment practices, they received performance incentives. This situation goes way beyond greed; this represents a grievous sin against the soul of the American people.

Greed is not just practiced by the leaders of our businesses and institutions; it is pervasive in our country and culture. It exists at all levels of our society. There are those who want something for nothing and collect all types of government assistance, but are quite capable of working, and there are those who try to cheat and take advantage of the old and poor. There are millions of Americans who operate in the comforting shadow of greed. They lie and cheat anybody they can to advance their lot in life and use deceitful practices to take every dishonest advantage with anyone they come in contact with.

I am not condemning all people on government assistance. There are many less fortunate people who, for many reasons, are not able to work and who should get the assistance they need to have a quality life. I am referring to the people who consistently try to cheat and scam the system. We all have heard stories on our local radio stations about people who have cheated the welfare system or Medicaid/Medicare system for years. Many of the Medicare/Medicaid cheats have been doctors and health-care organizations trying to maximize their profits. Most of us probably know someone who has collected benefits and is capable of working or may be working under the table. These individuals are quite able to get a job or go back to work after an alleged injury, but decide to stay on the dole and receive their SSI or workers' comp check while they participate in the food stamp program (there are currently over forty million people taking advantage of the food stamp program). They could work if they wanted to, but it is much easier to cheat and scam the system. Why go to work and earn an honest living when Uncle Sam will pay you almost the same amount of money?

When a salesperson tries to cheat you; when people sue others with frivolous lawsuits in the hope of a settlement versus a trial, where their claims would be denied or thrown out of court; when people steal hours from their employers by not working when they are supposed to be on the job; when employees falsify their time cards or expense reports—these are all forms of greed. Let's not forget those employees who take an inordinate number of days off due to an alleged illness, but in fact are not sick at all, or those who do just enough work not to get fired.

You can cheat on a test, you can cheat the government, you can cheat your employer, you can cheat on your spouse, you can cheat a friend or neighbor, you can cheat your customers—you can basically cheat anyone you desire to cheat. Many Americans do…and they don't think it is wrong. It is becoming the new norm of behavior for too many of our citizens. Just remember this: in life's journey, the scales of justice balance. It may take years, or even decades, but what you do to others in your life's transactions will eventually catch up with you and the scales will balance. Maybe it will be as simple as the people that have trusted, loved, or respected you abandoning you during your hour of greatest need. Maybe you will get fired from your job, lose your business, be cheated yourself—or worse, maybe you will lose the tender love and caring of the spouse or friends that have stood by while you violated their trust, support, friendship, and love. You might die a lonely and bitter soul.

Free Speech, Our Flag, Values, and God

It is time we move from greed to a more basic foundational concept: free speech. Let's take a look at the First Amendment according to some of our various legal groups, including our judges. We have the right to free speech. We have the right to be heard without being censored. However, I don't believe we should have the right to burn or desecrate our flag that so many of our young men and women sacrificed their lives defending, and, in some parts of the world, are dying while defending what our flag stands for and represents.

Should pornographers have the right to poison the minds of our children? Should organizations that advocate sex between adult men and young boys have their rights protected? If we could bring our founding fathers back from their graves to our world today, would they author a document that is different from the one they created in 1776? I don't think so, and I believe they would scold us for misinterpreting the meaning of their words.

Why don't we drastically restrict access to pornography on the Internet? Why don't we emphasize personal integrity, morality, and ethics more often in our schools, universities, and businesses? Why don't we severely punish rapists of young children, and those who have multiple charges of rape against women? Why do we wait until one of these perverts kills a child or a young woman?

What is our preoccupation with purging God from our schools and societal events? What is wrong with a movement to reestablish prayer in our classrooms? Is prayer so offensive and detrimental that it will cause psychological damage to our children? A teacher can put a condom on a banana but cannot put God in the hearts and minds of our children during class.

Why not teach values in school? Some of you may be thinking, "Whose values are you going to teach, and what if some students have a different value set?" My response to this line of thinking is: Why don't we start with the core set of values that were part of the fabric of our young nation over two hundred years ago? Why not teach the following values?

- *Respect*
- *Loyalty*
- *Honesty*
- *Integrity*
- *Hard work*
- *Dedication*
- *Commitment*
- *Sharing*
- *Helping others*

This is a simple list of what should be viewed as universal values to guide behavior in any culture. There are many more values that are important, but what is wrong with this list as a starting point?

I would like to state up front that there is nothing wrong with age-appropriate and responsible sex education presented by competent teachers. I would hope that it would have an impact on reducing teen-age pregnancies and sexually transmitted diseases. However, if we can teach middle-school students about sex, if we can demonstrate putting a condom on a banana, if we can teach birth control methods to children this age, why can't we teach them about respecting others, personal integrity, commitment, and hard work? Why can't we talk about God? Why can't we have a Christmas tree or a Christmas play anymore? We are focusing on the wrong things. For instance, it is okay to talk about sex education, but it is not okay to wish someone a merry Christmas.

It is not right that in the name of being politically correct, we ignore the feelings, needs, and desires of the silent majority and cater to the feelings of a radical few whom we don't want to offend. However, we will offend the majority of the people in our communities and disrespect their needs, desires, and wishes to placate the loud and obnoxious voices of a few selfish individuals with a personal agenda.

It is my strong belief that if there were more emphasis in our country on values, religion, and the various gods of the major religions, there would be a profound positive impact on the behavior of future generations of adults in the United States. I also believe that teenage pregnancy would decline significantly and high school dropout rates, especially those of our minority students, would fall rapidly. Personal integrity and honesty would reassert itself in our academic, government, and business communities and relationships. I deeply believe that there would be a greater appreciation of diversity, a more willing attitude to help those in need, and an increased kindness to others, regardless of their lot in life or backgrounds. In the long term, I think we would see a significant reduction of corruption in our government officials and business leaders.

For people who do not believe in a god or have no affiliation with a religion, this is not a problem, because the values that our founding fathers espoused and the values I have listed above are universal in their association to all mankind and apply to everyone in our country.

- Wouldn't you like to see the prison population in the United States decrease, especially the number of black and Hispanic young men?
- Wouldn't you like to see our elected representatives demonstrate a higher order of personal integrity?
- Wouldn't you like to see our business and union leaders operate with a greater amount of openness and honesty in their transactions?
- Wouldn't it be great for our entertainers and sports stars to be outstanding role models for our youth to emulate?
- Wouldn't it be great to know that our young men and women embodied truth and decency in their interactions?

All of these are possible if we embrace a value-driven philosophy throughout our society. A society that does not embrace a set of core operating principles will produce misfits and socially irresponsible, self-centered, greedy, uncaring citizens. How could you argue that the following values are not an appropriate way to behave and conduct your life?

- *Respect*
- *Loyalty*

- *Honesty*
- *Integrity*
- *Hard work*
- *Dedication*
- *Commitment*
- *Sharing*
- *Helping others*

These values are the basic core elements of how we should treat each other, regardless of whether we believe in a god, Mother Nature, some other force in the universe, or just ourselves. If you disagree with these core universal values, then what will you espouse as your central theme in life regarding how you behave, treat others, and function in our society? What would your values look like?

- If you could not embrace respect, would you be disrespectful to others?
- If you could not demonstrate loyalty, would you be disloyal to your family, friends, and employer?
- If you could not embrace honesty, would you lie and cheat your way through life?
- If you could not model integrity, would you allow yourself to engage in inappropriate behavior?
- If you could not work hard, would you be a slacker and have others do your share?
- If you could not be dedicated, would you go through life without a purpose and sense of meaning?
- If you could not exercise commitment, would your word and handshake mean nothing in life's transactions?
- If you could not share, would you hoard?
- Finally, if you would not help others, would you become consumed with satisfying yourself?

These are not the values of any one particular religion; instead, they represent universal values that frame how people should treat others and conduct their lives on this earth. These are the values that need to be reinforced in our schools, religious institutions, businesses, government organizations, and generally throughout the core of our society.

Chapter 5

Our Citizens and Social System

There is a dark cloud over our country and it is spreading its destructive energy. We don't care about each other the way people used to a century or two ago. Life has become cheap, and someone else's property a target for theft. Violence fills the minds of our children on a daily basis. I jotted down some notes over the years to reinforce the point that the sanctity of life has been lessened and the failure to strongly punish the doers of evil has created more evil. The failure of the family as a core unit in our society, the failure of our government, the failure of our kindergarten through twelfth-grade educational system, and the deterioration of our moral compass have all contributed to a lack of caring and concern for the well-being of our neighbors and citizens.

Let's look at some examples I have collected from headlines of various media sources to reinforce this point:

- A sweet, beautiful little girl, Caylee Anthony, was murdered and thrown away like garbage in a trash bag.
- A three-year-old girl was shot and killed in Los Angeles going down a blind alley by mistake.
- An Irish girl was killed in Boston with a knife—for no reason.
- An assistant district attorney was assassinated by a young black teenager because he was prosecuting a gang member.
- A young woman was murdered by her husband. Her heart and lungs were cut out in protest of their child's birth defects. Her husband was an executive for a major insurance company.
- In Indiana, a young woman's car was hit by a truck speeding through a stop sign. As she lay dying, passersby looted her

car and stole her credit cards and money from her purse. Nobody bothered to help her.

- A young woman was brutally beaten and raped. Both her arms were cut off and she was left for dead by the side of the road. After spending a few years in jail, her assailant was released for good behavior. He then turned around and complained that his civil rights were being violated because members of the community were complaining that he had moved into their neighborhood.
- Two beautiful little boys strapped into their car seats drowned in a car because their mother did not want to jeopardize her relationship with her lover, who did not want responsibility for the children.
- There have been a number of killings of police officers in the line of duty by career criminals with arrest records a mile long.
- A young gay man was tied to a fence and beaten to death just because he was gay.
- An African-American man was tied to the back of a pickup truck and dragged to his death just because he was black.
- Finally, there are all the school shootings that have taken place during the past ten years.

I have given enough examples in this particular area; if you want more, just tune in to the nightly cable news and you will hear these tales of horror during every newscast.

But what happens when these criminals are caught? You often hear what a difficult childhood they had. They claim they were abused and lived in a cycle of poverty, never knew their father, etc. They say they deserve a chance to be rehabilitated.

I say no, they should be executed. The perverts who kidnap, rape, and murder our children should forfeit their lives. It is time to stop the madness. How many more little boys and girls have to be tortured to death before we get serious? Even when these criminals are convicted of the most heinous crimes, what happens? They go to prison and receive three good meals a day. There are recreational facilities to exercise in; they even have conjugal visitation rights in some prisons. Some prisoners become legal advocates for other inmates and clog an already overtaxed judicial system with frivolous lawsuits.

Let's examine the lack of caring for our fellow citizens from other points of view. This past Christmas, a Wal-Mart employee died of heart failure after he was trampled while trying to protect a pregnant woman who had been pushed to the ground during a mad rush of holiday shoppers wanting to buy cheap toys on Black Friday morning. Previously, I highlighted the fact that a lot of our citizens think nothing of lying, cheating, or stealing. There is a total focus on "what's in it for me?" by a good percentage of our populace. They are not willing to sacrifice, to go the extra mile to help someone else in need. They are not willing to give of themselves and volunteer to help the less fortunate. However, they will take and take and take. They see adversity as a roadblock that cannot be overcome. They look for the government, their employers, or others to solve their problems. They blame everyone and everything for the challenges they encounter in life. They deny accountability for their actions and blame others for their plight, as opposed to looking in the mirror and accepting responsibility for their actions or inaction. I could go on with example after example of where their personal greed and lack of consideration have caused significant pain to others.

A slightly different point will bring this chapter of sadness to a close. For you churchgoers, at the end of services all that love for one another goes right out the window in the church parking lot, where it becomes kill or be killed trying to jockey for position to get ahead of the crowds.

I have had the opportunity to see parents get into physical confrontations after a youth hockey game; a parent of one player told the parent of a player from the opposing team that the other's son constantly used cheap shots during the game. These two genteel mothers had to be physically separated.

Many of our citizens have lost their ability to respect others and their property. They have put themselves in the front of the line for self-satisfaction. It is all about them—their needs, their wants, their desires, their careers, their comfort—and they have no compassion for others.

It is so sad to see our once-great citizens go from barn-raising to barn-busting, to go from compassionate and caring neighbors to people critical of and condescending to others, to go from people who are walking in the path of light next to God to people walking in the shadow of evil. We are transforming our society from individuals who want to do good deeds for others to individuals who are driven by greed and engage in acts of dishonor against the members and organizations of our society.

Wouldn't it be nice if each of our citizens did one good deed a day to help someone less fortunate? Those acts of kindness would create a blanket of goodness over our great society. It would create a positive and energizing force, a feeling of purpose and meaning. The veil of negativity that spans our country would be lifted. A warm and caring feeling toward everyone, regardless of his or her situation, would be present in all our actions and institutions. Christians, Jews, Muslims, atheists, etc., would be living and working together, guided by our core values and principles. All people would be not only tolerated, but respected and included.

To continue to explore the dynamics of our citizens and social system, I would like to reacquaint you with the hard fact that a good number of our children are being raised in an environment filled with poverty, crime, dysfunctional family relationships, and, in a lot of cases, without a good male role model. Our prison system is overflowing with young black and Hispanic men and women. The large majority of those men and women were kissed with the curse of a perpetuating cycle of hopelessness, despair, and little or no opportunities, except those offered by a life of crime on the streets. These young people are destined to follow a path that will lead them to prison or an early death:

- *Their parents have failed them*
- *The educational system has failed them*
- *The business community has failed them*
- *The government has failed them*

- *Society in general has failed them*
- *And they have failed themselves*

A good percentage of these young men and women were born into dysfunctional families. Many of them were born to teenage mothers, with no father in their lives. They have grown up in neighborhoods filled with crime, drugs, and alcohol abuse. They have not been taught the social graces or values necessary to become a productive member of society. Instead, their values are those of the street. They are broken with despair, envious with rage, and their hearts are darkened by loneliness from a lack of love. They have been embraced by an undesirable element in our society.

They are overwhelmed by fear, and it gives them no quarter. Whether at home, in school, or on the playground, fear is always with them. Their hearts have been hardened by a lack of success and recognition. They not only envy society, they loathe it. Stealing is their reward in life. Drugs are what comfort their soul. By the time they realize that there are, in fact, opportunities for them, it is too late. The train of life has left them imprisoned in the station of despair.

This is our greatest social problem to solve and it is solvable. The answer is a very simple one; the application of the answer is almost impossible. To believe it can be solved, you must think that the impossible is possible, the unthinkable is doable, and that every one of our children has the capacity for success and the opportunity for a life of enjoyment and satisfaction.

The following is my simple but almost impossible solution:

- The creation and assimilation of a strong set of family values into all aspects of our culture
- The development of excellent pre-K through twelfth-grade educational systems (the best in the world)
- The guarantee of a good job with businesses and corporations locating offices and plants in our most disadvantaged cities and towns
- A judicial system that is just and rehabilitative in nature

To break the cycle of despair and darkness, we need to reestablish a strong sense of family and a traditional set of values. The government, community leaders, business leaders, and school officials can all play a major role in turning the situation around. We can invest in our inner cities. We can, if we choose, reengineer our schools. Finally, rather than sending jobs to China and India, we could send them to our poorest cities and towns, thereby raising the standard of living for the most deserving of our citizens.

Regarding families and schools, we need to apply a "tough love" philosophy to start the thinking process that a transformation is possible. Utilizing the school systems, we need to start an indoctrination process at a very early age. We should immerse our youngest in the core values I have mentioned previously throughout this book. As soon as a child is toilet-trained, he or she should participate in an early education process. At every opportunity, we should be reinforcing our country's core values and principles of behavior.

At the same time, we should reengineer the welfare system so that the amount of money a person would receive is fixed or capped. An example of this would be if a mother is on welfare and has X number of children, she should be paid Y. If she chooses to have additional children, she should not receive any additional money. All welfare mothers who exceed the allotted number of children will be given the option of free sterilization and will receive a monetary incentive after the procedure has been done. Any person receiving welfare must participate in a mandatory educational program designed to teach life and career/work skills. Those who are capable of working should perform some form of community service or work internship related to their skills and future career aspirations. Companies which sponsor work intern programs should receive a tax incentive.

Any woman under the age of eighteen who becomes pregnant must attend parenting classes if she is to receive any government benefits. Any male (non-spouse) who is responsible for impregnating an unmarried woman must participate in parenting classes and behavioral educational programs. Men of any age who are responsible for impregnating more than three unmarried women should be required to have a vasectomy. Of course, these things will not happen, but that is the type of tough love we need to institute to break this vicious cycle of poverty, crime, families without a father figure, and dysfunctional behavior.

Any persons on welfare for more than six months should be required to work or attend work-based training programs, unless they are disabled. The government should give them a hand in life, not a perpetual handout.

As stated, we should reengineer our educational system. To address this particular social problem, every child under the age of eighteen should be required to attend school. A mandatory, highly structured and discipline-oriented educational alternative should be made available for students who consistently cause trouble in school. A higher-focused vocational program should be available for students who either lack the aptitude or desire to pursue a more academically focused educational track. However, every additional track will offer technology-based training. The goal of the highly structured and disciplined educational alternative is to reintegrate the problem students back into the vocational, academic, or business track educational systems as soon as possible.

Another strategic driving force to address these key social issues is providing our citizens with good jobs that are accessible to the poorest communities. This can be accomplished in a variety of ways. The first—and by far the best—method is to create enterprise zones within our poorest communities. The government should create a tax incentive for any company which will come into the neighborhood enterprise zone and either build a new facility or refurbish an existing facility/building. Companies that make this level of commitment should receive a tax-free status from the federal, state, and local governments for a period of twenty years. Extra incentives should be offered to companies that bring back jobs they have outsourced to overseas countries. It is time we bring American jobs back to America and provide the most disadvantaged among us an opportunity for a well-paying job, and an opportunity to learn skills and enjoy a successful career. It is time that we rebuild our inner-city neighborhoods and stop building neighborhoods in other parts of the world. During this economic downturn, it is time to invest in America.

Coupled with enterprise zones, but able to stand alone, would be tax incentives for any company that hires and transports people from an impoverished area to its organization for full-time employment opportunities. Job-training incentives should also be given to such companies to train these new workers with the appropriate skill sets.

The most difficult solution, which will only partially address this employment situation, is to create a transportation infrastructure for transporting people from the poorest areas to areas that have been developed as business centers. This will limit the number of targeted business centers. For example, if a city could extend a bus line or create a new route that would link an inner-city community with an established business complex that was previously accessible only by car, it would open up employment opportunities for the unemployed in the inner-city community.

Furthermore, it is time to reengineer our prison system with a new vision for rehabilitation. Our prisons need to be run like educational boot camps. Every prisoner should be trained in several different vocational skills/competencies, except prisoners who have less than one year to serve. These prisoners should go through training similar to that of military recruits, as well as having a heavy educational component on appropriate social and behavior skills.

Our prisons need to become work and educational centers of excellence focused on educating and shaping the behavior of prisoners for reentry into the community with the necessary skills and social acumen to be successful. For those prisoners who are recalcitrant, their privileges should be revoked and should will be required to perform hard physical work. Education should be mandatory for all prisoners, with the goal of receiving a GED and moving through a vocational/community college that will lead to a degree. Prisoners who happen to have a college degree will still be required to pass through the vocational educational track, although they may become teacher-certified to actually teach in this system.

The creation of enterprise prisons for inmates who can be trusted should be established. These prisons could represent the possibility of becoming potential repair depots for industrial electronics. Everything from call center operations to manufacturing could be part of the work provided by these enterprise prisoners. They would be paid a salary, and the prisons would earn profits on sales or services they provide.

Additionally, the prison system should have a professional and educational career progression tier-level system. Based on good behavior and educational performance, a prisoner could move up the tiered system. Hardcore, recalcitrant prisoners who cannot be rehabilitated would endure a life of hard work, discipline, structure, and few amenities. No more cable TV, no more gym, no more social time in the yard. There would be hard work and education until the person's behavior demonstrated a promotion to a higher tier level. The days of the very long rap sheet and multiple arrests would be over. The days of the rapists, murders, and robbers out on bail and able to commit more crimes would end. Strict and swift sentencing would be handed out; no more twenty years on death row.

We should use DNA as the conclusive arbitrator and redesign the appeals process, so if a prisoner is convicted of a death-sentence crime based on crime-scene DNA, he or she would be executed within a five-year period. Also requiring a redesign are the bail, sentencing, and parole systems. There should be swift and strict mandatory sentencing that would act as a deterrent. Parole should be based on educational and skill development performance, as well as behavior. If a prisoner has not participated in the educational and the work-skills development programs that are offered, he or she would not be eligible for parole. If a prisoner violates parole, he or she should be sent to a lower-tier institution and have to work back up the tier ladder.

There should be no more country-club prisons for the rich and powerful. Executives and politicians should be assigned to an enterprise prison, where they will work like everyone else. There should be no special privileges. White-collar crimes have deeply hurt tens of thousands of our citizens. Just look at the damage, pain, and suffering that executives in organizations such as Enron and WorldCom created for our citizens. Families lost their entire life savings as a result of the actions of a few greedy Wall Street investors and bankers who made tens of millions of dollars in bonuses. Some politicians have gotten rich at the expense of their constituents. They thought of only themselves as they hobnobbed with greedy special interest groups and lobbyists. The people who elected them to represent their best interests and the best interests of their communities were not invited to the table of power; rather, they were forgotten in a sea of deception.

It is very possible to once again develop a society of people who care for each other and are willing to help advance the standard of living and the quality of life for all Americans. We can, and I believe we will, continue to create the greatest society on the planet if we embrace the necessary reforms to bring the pendulum back to the center of American life.

Chapter 6

Our Political System

The 2008 election process took over two years to select the Republican and Democratic presidential candidates and to elect Barack Obama as our forty-fourth president. What transpired during those two years and what continues to be the acceptable norm of behavior for both parties represents a microcosm of how our political system works. Quite frankly, it doesn't. We have a dysfunctional government influenced more by the rich and powerful and Washington lobbyists than by the average American citizens who live by the rules. Average American citizens work hard and try to do the best they can to raise their families. They vote to send elected officials to Congress to represent their current interests and the future welfare of their children. However, what really happens?

The people they elect, either Republicans or Democrats, arrive in Congress and are assimilated into a code of conduct that is adversarial toward the opposing party. They are then harassed by a deluge of special interest groups and high-paid lobbyists. Some forget who elected and sent them to Congress to serve the best interests of their state and country. Instead, a few start to operate in the best interest of their political parties and special interest groups that have contributed to their election campaigns. Those individuals are driven by greed, power, and influence, and they become corrupt. Many of them lie and cheat the very country and constituents they are supposed to represent.

Spending orgies, pork-barrel projects, and supporting legislation that has been developed by lobbyists become standard operating procedure. These corrupt and arrogant politicians demonstrate a lack of concern for America and the American workers.

- They have created a bloated, ineffective, non-value-added bureaucratic government
- They fund programs that don't make any sense and don't add value to our way of life
- They develop laws, policies, and regulations that put us at a competitive disadvantage in the global marketplace
- They make it difficult for small businesses to grow and expand
- They develop pages and pages of forms to be completed by our citizens and make the simple complicated, and the complicated impossible
- There is no sense of service to the American citizen, no sense of fairness, no accountability on the part of government employees, no commitment to providing an excellent level of customer service to our citizens

But those are not really the big problem. The most significant behavioral problem that our elected officials ignore is simply their ability to engage in healthy debate, discourse, or disagreements without an ugly attack on individuals or political ideology. During the 2008 election, candidates were on every major cable network.

- They distorted the position of candidates with a constant stream of lies, half-truths, and misrepresentations
- They made false assumptions and took out of context what the other person said
- They put negative spins on what the other candidates said, did, or stood for regarding their positions
- They operated with mean, hateful, and dishonest intentions
- They stooped very low to hurt the other candidates and their family members
- With great indignation, arrogance, and uncontrolled egos, they engaged in a "scorched earth" approach to destroy the other candidates and their political parties
- They polarized the American voters with a senseless diatribe of lies and misstated facts

Even the media, which is supposed to remain neutral, failed to maintain its objectivity and engaged in perpetuating these politically polarizing behaviors. But it did not stop there; when average American citizens came together in what is known as a Tea Party to protest the health-care reform bill, they were attacked by the same politicians they sent to Washington to represent them. They were accused of being unpatriotic, un-American radicals, and, by a few, racist. In my view, these were good, loyal, and decent Americans who disagreed with the health-care reform legislation. Many of them only wanted Congress to start over with a clean slate and include the voice of the people in the process. Many even agreed that reform is necessary but wanted a slower approach. Some just wanted Congress and President Obama to read the 2,500-page bill to fully understand the consequences before passing the legislation. Others want tort reform and a crackdown on the blatant Medicare and Medicaid fraud first, and then to tackle the other areas of health-care reform. And yes, some want to kill the bill.

What happened was an example of an abuse of power by our elected government officials. Not only was the will of the majority of American citizens ignored regarding their disagreement and displeasure with the way the health-care reform legislation was created, congressional leaders and White House officials verbally attacked those who opposed their decision as being radicals and un-American. This just underscores the arrogance of some of our governmental officials. Whatever happened to constructive political discourse and debate?

What is the solution to this quagmire of deceit, dishonesty, and unprofessional behavior? It is simply the establishment of a viable third political party founded on the principles and values that have made this a great country. We need a strong third party, a party with candidates driven by duty, honor, integrity, and serving the best interests of their states and our nation. We need a third party that will be willing to eliminate the staggering bureaucracy in Washington, a party that will streamline policies and procedures that currently inflict pain and suffering on many of our fellow citizens. We need a party we can trust and a party that will demonstrate trustworthy behavior. We need a party with elected officials that will work in the best interests of their state and nation, and not in serve lobbyists or focus on their personal agenda for wealth and power. We need to reengineer the role of federal government and bring it back into alignment with the vision of our founding fathers.

Every program should be highly scrutinized regarding whether it is absolutely necessary to be administered by the federal government. There are three questions that should be asked: 1) Is the program absolutely necessary? If the answer is no, we should get rid of it. In regard to the elimination of government programs, the citizens should be able to vote on whether or not they want it. If the program cannot be eliminated, then we need to ask: 2) Can the program be substantially improved (reengineered) or sent to the state governments to be administered? The final question we should ask of each program is: 3) Whom does it benefit? If the program does not benefit the majority of the legal citizens of the United States and it is not mission-critical, we should get rid of it. We should establish a national goal that reduces the size of our federal government by 30 percent in five years.

This national goal should also include the consolidation of programs and agencies that are providing similar or redundant programs and services. If we can put a man on the moon ten years after President Kennedy established the goals for space exploration, we can certainly downsize the federal government by 30 percent within five years. This can be accomplished through the use of advanced, performance-based administrative technologies, elimination of redundancy, procedural redesigns, process improvements, and the elimination of non-value-added work.

Another basic idea for improving the performance of our government officials would be the establishment of a simple set of operating principles or values, along with a set of significant consequences for any government officials who violate those principles. In addition, those operating principles and consequences should be applied to any lobbyist, businessperson, individual, or organization that is soliciting business or influence from any government officials. Too many special deals, pork projects, and influence by lobbyists and special interest groups go unchecked in today's government.

Finally, every bill should stand on its own. There should be no earmarks or add-ons of any kind: one item, one bill. The line item veto should be a standard tool that the president uses to ensure that all the elements of a bill will add value to the American people and the nation in general.

Here is an example of earmarks as reported by Paul Kane on February 17, 2010, in the *Washington Post*:

By Paul Kane

Congress devoted nearly $16 billion to line-item spending this year, decreasing the overall number of so-called earmarks that lawmakers issued but spending slightly more on those controversial items in President Obama's first year in office.

For fiscal 2010, Congress included 9,413 earmarks in the annual appropriations bills that fund the federal government, down from 10,363 in 2009, according to a report released Wednesday by Taxpayers for Common Sense, an independent watchdog dedicated to routing out waste. Those earmarks – which Obama has vowed to sharply reduce – accounted for $15.9 billion, up from $15.6 billion last year. (Kane, 2010)

Isn't it sad that both our Republican and Democrat lawmakers have a total disregard for balancing the budget? They are more interested in their special projects than standing tall and saying, "Enough wasteful government spending. There will be no more earmarks." No, they won't say it because they need to bring home the bacon to ensure that they get reelected. They need to give back to the people who have contributed to their campaigns. They have IOUs to honor with special interest groups and lobbyists. While they spend your children's future and pontificate about how the other party is wasting your money, they quietly add their pork items to various forms of legislation.

The fundamental core platform elements of the third political party should be small government, less spending, a values-driven orientation, an uncompromising desire to honor our national traditions and customs while respecting the diversity of our population, a commitment to improving the quality of life for all Americans, and an absolute dedication to provide all citizens with respectful and responsive programs and services.

As a country, we should create an ideal vision of the future for our government. This vision should include world leadership in the areas of education, science and technology, environmentalism, medicine, agriculture production, and manufacturing. To support this vision of our ideal future, we will need a set of national operating values to act as the beacon to light our path as a nation in our quest for sustainable greatness in the world community.

While we spend our children's future on frivolous and bloated government programs and agencies that do not add value, China and India grow with a sense of purpose, pride, and long-term vision. Their people have been energized by their political leaders. They can see prosperity. We, on the other hand, have been disillusioned, disenfranchised, and disempowered by the fraudulent behavior of our political leaders. It is absolutely essential that we reverse this polarizing trend that currently exists between the Republican and Democratic parties.

If we are to survive the onslaught of global competition, we will require a new dimension of political leadership. It is time that we reengineer our federal government or accept mediocrity as a nation of people who could have had sustained greatness, but instead chose greed, comfort, and entitlement.

Chapter 7

Our Educational System

As with our federal government, our educational system is broken. It has not functioned very well since it was liberalized in the '60s and '70s. Some teachers and administrators will ignore bullying and drugs and will allow students to come to school dressed like slobs and gang members. They will allow young girls to dress inappropriately, but will not push for uniform dress standards.

I attended Catholic grammar and high schools. The discipline was tough and the level of structure was high. I wore a shirt and tie every day, even in the hot weather. If you got out of line, you were disciplined. I had the unfortunate pleasure of having my ears pulled and knuckles rapped with a ruler many times. We drilled our math tables each day and chanted our spelling words. There was a tension and fear of authority, but a healthy respect for the teachers and administrators.

Today's kids go to school looking like slobs. There is little respect for teachers, administrators, or staff. The traditional values that were taught in the classrooms of my day have been replaced by sex education. Instead of positive stories about the family, those have been modified to focus on alternative family structures. Both sex education and discussing diversity issues are necessary at the appropriate grade level and with qualified and unbiased teachers presenting the subject matter. But let's make sure there is balance in the classroom, and discuss the importance of living your life guided by values and principles.

In the name of political correctness, our traditional holiday celebrations have been eliminated. This past Christmas, I went to a school concert that my granddaughter was in, and to my surprise and disbelief, they did not sing any Christmas carols. Actually, they did not call it as a "Christmas" play. There was an absence of any signs or symbols that would refer to Christmas: no Christmas tree or decorations of any kind. When I asked my daughter why, she told me that the school system did not want to offend anyone, especially people who did not believe in Christ or celebrate Christmas. So, the majority of the people in this school system were denied an opportunity to express their holiday tradition because the administrators did not want to offend a small minority. However, we will subject 100 percent of the children to sex education. We will talk about how it is okay to live an alternative lifestyle and commit to an alternate form of marriage, but it is not okay to mention Christmas or sing a traditional carol.

In addition to being overly politically correct, compared to many other developed nations in the world, we are way behind in math and science. We are graduating some kids from high school who cannot read beyond the fifth-grade level and who can barely make change while working a cash register.

Furthermore, some of the decisions school administrators are making just don't make any sense. For instance, we have an obesity crisis among our children and a lot of schools have eliminated gym classes. After-school intramural sports programs have been eliminated or substantially reduced. You cannot even have a game of tag in some schools due to a zero tolerance for touching. Some school districts have instituted a no-touch policy and have disciplined a few children for playing tag. When I was a kid, we would play tag for hours at a time and get a lot of very good exercise, in addition to strengthening problem-solving and decision-making skills, and learning teamwork.

We can pay school administrators six-figure incomes, and we can create a very large bureaucracy, but we do not pay our young and very bright teachers more than the starting salary of a manager at McDonald's. We allow students to be belligerent and condescending to teachers and refuse to back teachers when they take a stand. We promote students to the next grade when they have not met the requirements of the current grade. Teachers' unions block real reforms at every turn and protect teachers who are poor performers. Why do the teachers' unions in some school systems throughout the United States fight real reforms? Why do they protect ineffective teachers from being disciplined or fired? The answer is simply greed. Just follow the money.

A number of the leaders of teachers' unions throughout the United States are more concerned about the size of their membership, the union dues they will collect, and the amount of power they wield than they are about the students their members serve. That is right, I said serve. We need to shift the paradigm to look at students as our customers and approach these young people from the standpoint of how best to serve them and meet their needs, while providing them with a world-class educational experience.

We need to set a goal to become the most educated country in the world—not India, not China, not Ireland, not Japan, but the United States. Also, teachers must be held accountable for performance. Tenure must end, or we must at least incorporate a performance-based review every two years, and advancement must be based on results. The administrative functions in schools must be de-layered and reduced. It should be a requirement that every administrator in a management position teach one course during a school year. This will ground the bureaucrats and keep them in touch with what goes on in the classroom. And we should institute pay-for-performance for all teachers and school administrators, based on the test scores and accomplishments of their students.

There should be standards for membership on a school board. We need some of the best and brightest parents and most successful business leaders on school boards. It should not be a popularity contest. Therefore, I propose a committee be formed to select new school board members based on a pre-established set of standards. This selection committee should be composed of school principals, town leaders, PTA members, business leaders, and concerned citizens to serve the needs of the students, not their personal agendas. Also, students should be represented by members of the honor society.

If we are to achieve the goal of being the most educated nation in the world, we also will need to become the most technologically proficient society in the world. It may sound old-fashioned, but we need to get back to the core basics of reading, writing, and arithmetic. We need to emphasize math, science, language, and the arts. We need to focus more on critical thinking skills and less on sexuality. In addition, every student entering middle school should be given a computer, and all classes should utilize technology in their curriculum. Every student in elementary school should be taught the basics of how to use a computer for research. Homework assignments should contain an online component.

For students who have a more technical aptitude, we need to redesign our vocational programs to focus on current and future technologies and technical career fields. We should spend more time on science. Instead of baking in home economics, we should spend more time on biotechnology. Instead of free study time, we should spend more study time on foreign languages. Starting in first grade, all students should be taught a foreign language. By the time a student graduates from high school, he or she should be proficient in one foreign language. We should make it mandatory that every student plays one intramural sport each semester.

Finally, we should make a commitment to our children that all who graduate from high school will have the opportunity to go on to a four-year college, community college, or technical school if they so chose. Tuition assistance should be made available for any adult who goes back to school while on the job.

A good education is the cure for a lot of our social problems. Education will lead to a reduction in crime, fewer of our young minority men in prison, good jobs for more of our at-risk young men, fewer teenage pregnancies, stronger family-oriented values, a more innovative and productive workforce, more opportunities for our citizens to make their dreams come true, and a stronger competitive position in the global marketplace.

To sum up, all children from grades one through twelve should be constantly exposed to our national core values and principles. A social community-based project should be included in every grade each school year. Major emphasis should be placed on the development of individual and team academic projects that will create a constructive level of competition within the school environment. If we are going to successfully compete in this twenty-first-century global economy, we ought to create a spirit of healthy and constructive competition between classes and academic teams. Yes, it is true that Johnny and

Sue might not take first place, but they will learn how to compete and win at their level of competence.

What is our alternative? We can sit back and let China, Brazil, Mexico, India, Korea, and Japan continue to take our jobs and steal our future, or we could start to re-ignite the spirit of America through a new generation of innovative American students.

If you still think we have the best educational system in the world, take a moment to reflect upon the following results of an international comparisons in math, reading, and science among fifteen-year-olds that was developed by the Organization for Economic Co-operation and Development's Program for Student Assessment. More than 250,000 fifteen-year-old students from forty-one countries participated in the assessment. The countries included all major industrialized nations (results for Britain were not available) and eleven other nations that chose to participate. The test scores are from 2003.

Mean performance on the mathematics scale - The United States ranked 25th

Mean performance on the reading scale – The United States ranked 12th

Mean performance on the science scale – The United States ranked 20th

The following was taken from an article written by Heather Chikoore:

Experts believe that in order for America to remain an economic leader in a global economy we must ensure that our citizens have strong skills in science, technology, engineering and math. Yet international comparisons of student achievement in math and science intensify concern about the United States' ability to remain competitive. The 2006 Program for International Student Assessment indicates that American 15-year-olds test 21ˢᵗ among 30 developed countries on science literacy and 25ᵗʰ on math literacy.[1]

We must get serious about educational reform if we are to maintain our superior status in the community of nations. For it is the United States which has a track record of leadership, compassion, giving, and fairness in dealing with other nations, and if we fall behind because we have a subpar educational system, the world will suffer a great deal of hardship and pain. The United States has been the leader in science, medicine, agriculture, engineering, transportation, and manufacturing, and our educational system has been the driving engine for our success in the past. It will be the driving force for our failure in the future if we do not change it.

Do you want this great nation of ours to maintain its high school graduation rate of twenty-third in the world's industrialized communities? Should we continue to graduate more lawyers per capita while China and India graduate more scientists and engineers? We can continue with the highest level of litigation in the world, or we can allow our young engineers and scientists to create wealth for our nation as a result of their inventiveness. However, to develop a new model of education for our kindergarten through twelfth-grade students will require a new dimension of leadership in our government and educational administrators.

A big infrastructure sore our country is experiencing is the number of our inner-city schools that are in desperate need of repairs and technological upgrades. We are building schools in other parts of the world; why not build schools that will allow our children to learn and be able to compete on a level playing field in the global economy?

By the way, I thought you might like to know that Japan, who happens to be one of our major global competitors, is experimenting with putting computer workstations on some of their school buses so students can utilize the time while they are being transported to school researching and doing assignments.

_____

1

In the United States, we have put guards on a few of our school buses. Children have been beaten on some. Lesson learned: if we want to maintain a competitive position in the global marketplace, we need to reform our educational system. China, India, and the European Union (EU) will take no prisoners on the marketplace battlefield of products and services. The key for the United States to maintain its global leadership and prevent itself from becoming a third-world country is a world-class education for our children.

Chapter 8

Our Infrastructure

The "death of the American heart" has had catastrophic consequences on our infrastructure. We are giving billions of dollars a year to other nations around the world so they can rebuild their infrastructure. Isn't it about time we got serious and started to rebuild our own? However, in doing so, we need to learn a lesson from the "Big Dig" in Boston. This was a two-billion-dollar infrastructure project that ballooned to over fifteen billion dollars when it was completed because of greed, corruption, and mismanagement! There is plenty of blame to go around, and you will find the same cast of characters at the taxpayers' feeding trough; namely, local politicians, corrupt managers, union leaders, and dishonest vendors. However, with good, ethical, and visionary leadership, we can rebuild our infrastructure and substantially improve the quality of life for all Americans.

Go to Germany, Japan, France, and China and you will find high-speed rail systems that are fast, reliable, comfortable, and an enjoyable form of transportation. In contrast, every major city in the United States is experiencing big issues in trying to deal with too many cars during the morning and afternoon commuter rush hours. Whether it is Los Angeles or Boston, Las Vegas or Baltimore, if you are commuting any distance to work by car, plan on spending a lot of time sitting in stop-and-go traffic. Because of the financial meltdown, our poorly performing economy, and the excessively high unemployment rate as a result of outsourcing jobs to China and India, most of our cities and larger towns lack the necessary resources to adequately fix transportation and other infrastructure problems. I encourage you to look around as you travel through the cities and towns of the United States and note the number of decaying buildings, office complexes, and manufacturing plants. Where we have experienced outsourcing, you will see structural decay and abandoned buildings. Here is an example of what is happening throughout the United States:

International Paper's Franklin plant to close
October 22, 2009 1:49 pm.

International Paper announced Thursday it would close its paper mill in Franklin by spring of next year, putting 1,100 people out of work.

The Memphis, Tenn.-based company said the closure was necessary because the demand for uncoated free-sheet paper had declined during the global recession.

"We recognize these are very difficult decisions affecting our employees, their families and the communities surrounding these mills," International Paper Chairman and CEO John Faraci said in a statement. "We have concluded that we have excess capacity in our North American paper and packaging businesses, and these decisions will better match our supply with our expected customer demand."

The company also announced it would close its containerboard mills in Pineville, La., and Albany, Ore., cutting another 500 jobs. Gov. Timothy M. Kaine said he has commissioned the Virginia Employment Commission to create an Economic Crisis Strike Force to help displaced workers at the plant.

"International Paper's intended closing of its Franklin facility as part of planned actions nationwide is a deep blow to the community and the commonwealth," Kaine said in a statement. "This plant has long served as an economic asset for the area and its phased closing is most distressing. My heart goes out to the affected workers and their families, as well as all others who will be affected by this closure."

The company said salaried employees will be offered severance packages and outplacement assistance. It is working with union officials on severance benefits for hourly workers. (VirginiaBusiness.com, 2009)

International Paper to acquire Asian packaging business of Svenska Cellulosa

Posted on: Tues., 27 Apr 2010, 14:40:56 EDT

Apr 27, 2010 (Datamonitor Financial Deals Tracker via COMTEX)

International Paper Company (IPC), a US-based paper and packaging company, has entered into an agreement to acquire the Asian packaging business of Svenska Cellulosa Aktiebolaget SCA, a Sweden-based consumer goods and paper company, for $200 million in cash. The acquisition includes 15 plants in China, Singapore, Malaysia and Indonesia. The transaction is expected to close in the second quarter of 2010. (COMTEX, 2010)

So what is the point of these articles? They highlight the travesty that is happening in our manufacturing industry. We will close plants in the United States that will result in the entire community suffering a great loss of jobs and economic stability. The plant closing will cause a domino effect, forcing many of the small independent businesses that supported the plant and a number of vendors and suppliers to go out of business. The plant closing will have a significant negative impact on the tax base, which will start the process of infrastructural decay. At the same time, the companies that closed their plants in the United States will open new facilities in China, Mexico, Brazil, India, or other cheap-labor countries. The devastation of these communities is not a hypothetical situation. It is real and it is happening every day in our country.

For instance, I was traveling through the Midwest and happened to witness the aftermath of a major plant shutting down after years of being the economic engine for a community. Entire blocks of small mom-and-pop stores had closed. These stores had relied on the employees of this plant for their revenue, as did the town. Storefronts and windows were boarded up. It was like a ghost town. Nobody was around.

In addition to our failing infrastructure as a result of outsourcing, our facilities, roads, bridges, sewer and water systems, and electrical grids are in a state of perpetual rot. It is like our infrastructure is suffering from the worst case of terminal cancer, and greed is to blame. We have experienced major infrastructure failures in Minnesota, Connecticut, and Massachusetts. Whether it is bridges collapsing into rivers or a tunnel ceiling falling onto a car, if things do not change, we should count on more disasters occurring and more Americans dying.

I would look squarely in the eyes of our corporate leaders, union officials, and state, city, and town governments, and state unequivocally: you have failed the American people because of your greed and corruption. Compounded by your lack of vision for creating a better future, you have let your organizations, states, cities, towns, and the American people suffer. The consequences of your inaction and corrupt power-focused behavior started the vortex of decline for our great nation and its people. You failed to see the competitive threat from Japan. You failed to upgrade your facilities, operating processes, and staff competencies.

To our business leaders, you failed to modernize your operations. Instead, you opted for higher salaries, enormous bonuses, and lots of executive perks. For our union leaders, you became blinded by greed and power, and as a result created the forces of outsourcing that have taken root and flourished. You negotiated in the best interests of yourselves to maintain your hold on power, thereby forcing your companies to flee to cheaper labor markets, as opposed to modernizing and building new facilities in the United States.

You who have been elected by the citizens of our cities and towns would rather advance your petty personal agendas than initiate bold and creative actions necessary to sustain economic success and revitalization in your communities.

Drive around the Northeast during the winter months and you will be lucky not to have your car swallowed up by a giant pothole that should have been fixed but remains on the hunt for unsuspecting vehicles. They are to be avoided at all costs. Still, they are not fixed. The cost of failing to fix these potholes falls on the shoulders of the taxpayers through damaged tires and front-end alignments. By the way, during the morning and afternoon rush hour, our taxpaying citizens sit in bumper-to-bumper traffic trying to get to work or home.

Environmentalists think about all the carbon emissions being emitted into the atmosphere, as well as the millions of gallons of gas being wasted. The standard solution is to use public transportation or get a commuting partner and take the carpool lane. I am sorry to say, but in our country it does not work that way. In most cases, we do not have even an average public transportation system to access. In America, people tend to commute long distances to work, and depending on where they live, public transportation system options are very limited.

As I write this chapter, I am on a plane returning from a business trip to France. I used the public transportation system in France to go from the airport in Paris to the city of Lille. It was a very pleasant and convenient experience. In fact, one literally can go to almost any major city in Europe by train. There are a variety of transportation options. The morning I started to write this chapter, I checked out of my hotel in Lille, walked across the street, and five minutes later was on a train bound for the Charles de Gaulle Airport in Paris. During my career, I have traveled throughout Europe and Japan, using their train systems. Their trains are clean, very fast, and on time.

In the United States, it is very difficult to travel by train unless you are located near a station. Your only choice is to drive. Our train schedules are not robust like those of our European neighbors. Our trains are not as clean and our terminals smell. In some cases, they are not safe. Our roads are congested, our bridges are in dire need of repair, and our public transportation system needs a major overhaul and redesign. In addition, public transportation is very expensive. My wife, grandson, and I wanted to go to Washington, D.C., for a long weekend. At the time we were planning our trip, the train would have taken at least five times longer and cost more than flying from Boston.

Where are all our taxes going? We have federal, state, and local government taxes on gas, but our bridges are still in decay, our roads are overcrowded, and our public transportation system languishes behind those of other developed nations of the world. If Disney World can move tens of thousands of people around its parks every day with a transportation system that was built in the '70s, then we should be able to get our citizens to and from work without long delays or killing the planet.

Chapter 9

Our Global Role and the United Nations

Regarding our role in the world, America should stop policing and getting involved in every global conflict. First and foremost, the war in Europe is over. Actually, it has been over for approximately sixty-five years. An interesting question to ask ourselves is: why do we have military bases in most key European countries? The more interesting question is: why do we have military bases in about forty countries throughout the world?

You can talk all you want about our strategic interest, but is it really necessary to have all these military bases around the world? We are not at war with Germany, France, or Great Britain. So why have military bases in those countries? Why must we be first to send troops into a conflict in another country? Also, when we send American troops in response to a global conflict, we send the most. It seems like other countries send a mere pittance, and certainly not their fair share.

Here is what I recommend. Let's close 50 percent of our military bases overseas within the next ten years and redeploy those assets to the United States. While we are at it, why not relocate those assets in some of our poorest communities to stimulate job growth? If we can fly a drone aircraft over Afghanistan from a military base in the United States and launch a missile attack to kill the bad guys, I do not think we will be at such a disadvantage if we pull our troops out of Germany, France, Italy, and Great Britain. At the same time, we should demand that the United Nations step up and start to assume its core responsibilities for resolving global conflicts.

You are probably thinking I am crazy to think the United Nations is capable of or even willing to take the lead in resolving critical conflicts around the world. Given the current structure, operating philosophy, and behavior of the United Nations, in my opinion, its members operate as though they either lack the will, desire, motivation, and ability to be the world arbitrator of global disputes, or they just don't have the leadership within the U.N. structure to quickly respond to global conflicts. Simply defined, the United Nations appears to be a bloated, dishonest, do-nothing bureaucracy.

It has not taken the swift and decisive action required in some hot spots in the world, and has watched from the sidelines of humanity while genocide has taken place, without lifting a finger to help. People have been murdered and mutilated in front of U.N. troops. They have allowed these atrocities to take place because their charter was that of a peacekeeping force, and so as long as they are not attacked, they tend not to get involved in local or tribal-related issues. The U.N. issues sanctions that don't have any real teeth, and when a country that is in violation fails to comply with the policy, it will just issue additional sanctions. It is extremely difficult to get every one of the charter nations to agree on sanctions that would make a real difference. Case in point, Iran's nuclear development. Iranian leaders have stated that they will wipe Israel off the face of the earth, and according to all accounts they are trying to build a nuclear weapon. Given their association with terrorists groups and their statements about destroying Israel, it is only a matter of time before there is a global nuclear conflict. But the U.N. seems powerless to stop this from happening.

In many conflicts and human rights issue around the globe, basic decency and concern for human life would dictate that the U.N. get involved, but politics dictate that it does not get involved. So, people are murdered and tortured, women are raped, and children are enslaved in sex rings, but the U.N. seems to talk about these situations versus acting to stop them. I still do not know exactly why, based on a rumor of potential violence, the U.N. doctors and nurses abandoned a field hospital and left severely injured and dying Haitians during the recent earthquake. Sanjay Gupta, a CNN reporter and medical doctor, stayed with those Haitians until the following day, when the U.N. doctors returned. There have also been several allegations of corrupt U.N. officials. The following is taken from a report from TheTrumpet.com on October 20, 2005:

The Corruption of the United Nations

October 20, 2005, TheTrumpet.com

The oil-for-food scandal was an international embarrassment—but it's just one example in an organization rife with corruption.

Rape. Murder. Billions of dollars in fraud and embezzlement on a global scale. The United Nations, formed to "save succeeding generations from the scourge of war," has instead become more like a movie that is too graphic to show your children.

In the last few years, the reputation of the UN has been shredded by allegations of kickbacks, billions of dollars in graft in the oil-for-food scandal, the rape of minors in the Congo, sex scandal, and a significant lack of accountability. United Nations officials know it's time for serious reform.

The independent <u>report on the oil-for-food scandal</u>, produced by a committee led by former U.S. Federal Reserve Bank Chairman Paul Volcker, was finally released in September. Criticizing the UN from top to bottom, the language of the report was crystal clear: "The inescapable conclusion from the committee's work" is that the UN "needs thorough reform—and it needs it urgently." We will see exactly how serious the lapses in judgment were at every level. But with a goal as noble as saving our children from war, how did things go so terribly askew? What's wrong with the United Nations? (TheTrumpet.com, 2005)

One may question Trumpet.com as a source, but I would encourage you to take a side trip and use Google to search for "U.N. corruption" to see what comes up regarding the various articles on bribery and waste. In all fairness to the United Nations, it is trying to address the issue, but when over seventy countries in the world have been identified as corrupt, it is difficult to effectively manage the financial aid that is sent to them. Here is an article from Forbes.com:

SPECIAL REPORT

The World's Most Corrupt Countries

David A. Andelman 04.03.07, 6:00 PM ET

Corruption in nearly half the world's nations is not getting much better and, indeed, in many countries is intensifying—affecting virtually every aspect of life among peoples on every continent.

While a year ago, some 72 out of 158 nations surveyed by the international watchdog group Transparency International were classified as "corrupt," now 74 of 163 countries fall into the same category. A few, most notably India, managed to bootstrap themselves (just barely) out of the truly corrupt group, while others, particularly Iran, dug themselves more firmly into that camp. (Andelman, 2007)

Here is the list of the most corrupt nations as reported by Andelman in his article "The World's Most Corrupt Countries." The ratings were developed by Transparency International. The top ten are as follows:

#1 Haiti

The police continue to be a central factor in corruption in Haiti, though there is corruption in virtually every governmental body. Since the police are also the officials closest to every individual on a daily basis, it is their corruption that changes the nature of daily life in Haiti, permeating all society and the way business is done.

#2 Myanmar

Corruption is perceived as widespread in this vicious dictatorship run with an iron hand by a strong-willed clique of military leaders, who persist in repression of civil society at every level. Illicit facilitation payments and informal fees are required to access even the most basic government services.

#3 Iraq

Huge quantities of funds—especially American military and reconstruction aid funds—swirling through this nation, where many civil structures have largely broken down, is a recipe for corruption at all levels. Beyond kidnappings and ransom payments, TI officials say their survey was conducted in the first half of 2006, when funds being handled by the Coalition Provisional Authority were largely exhausted and no longer being disbursed. So the Iraqi government, where corruption is said to be rampant, was in charge of its own funds. International businessmen from a range of countries converging on Baghdad found finance, export credits, contracts, and a host of more mundane functions of government all subject to illicit payments.

#4 Guinea (Conakry)

Guinea has been in a political crisis state for at least three years. Though the current, corrupt president has been in power for twenty years, strong pressure has been building from the public for a change of regime. A public strike that lasted one month finally ended. There was outright civil strife, obliging the president to appoint a new prime minister. The most controversial, and corrupt, deals surround the mining sector, particularly aluminum. Among foreign businessmen, the general view, according to the TI survey, was that to do business in Guinea, you needed "to pay off the guy at the top."

#5 Sudan

The key event was the switch from a Canadian company that dominated oil drilling in Sudan, the number three oil producer in Africa, to a Chinese company that took over the contract after the Canadians found corruption, and an outrageous human rights record, was too rife to be able to continue functioning. China is now responsible for 90 percent of all oil production in Sudan, which also controls oil flow down a large pipeline through southern Sudan to the sea. Chinese officials have declined any comment on the human rights situation, and TI officials say they are "not too worried about having to pay off the Khartoum government."

#6 Democratic Republic of the Congo

Copper in Katanga, and in the rest of the country, gold, uranium, and especially coltan, a rare mineral that's in every cell phone chip, still drive the corruption that remains rampant in this African nation. A presidential election did little to stop the corruption or the resulting violence that erupted again in downtown Kinshasa, the nation's capital. The president is the principal recipient of routine payments by the mining companies, who apparently are prepared to play the very lucrative payoff game that remains as endemic now as it was back during the regime of one of Africa's historically most corrupt leaders, Mobutu Sese Seko.

#7 Chad

Chad has dropped from number one to number seven this year as international aid agencies, particularly the World Bank, have sought to come to grips with one of the world's most piggish uses of philanthropic funds. Proceeds of a Chad-Cameroon oil pipeline, funded in part by the World Bank and operated by an Exxon Mobil-led consortium, were supposed to have been used to help feed the desperately poor people of both nations. Instead, at least thirty million dollars was diverted to buy arms to keep the government of President Idriss Deby in power. The World Bank, whose president, Paul Wolfowitz, was deeply embarrassed by the fiasco, halted funding more than a year ago, but reached an accord with Chad last July. According to TI officials, the jury's still out on how effectively it will be implemented.

#8 Bangladesh

There continues to be a general lack of engagement between the government and civil society as repression and corruption throughout government ranks, and especially in the judiciary and political circles, persist, often spilling over into the private sector. In March, the new military-backed government jailed at least forty prominent business and government leaders from two of the leading political parties in what was described as an ongoing probe of corruption, but TI officials are little impressed. Still, after five straight years at the top of the list, Bangladesh has signed the United Nations convention against corruption and has now dropped to number eight.

#9 Uzbekistan

The most corrupt of the five former Soviet Republics on the list, Uzbekistan is sinking ever deeper into corruption and unrest—in constant turmoil and strife under what the U.S. State Department describes as the authoritarian rule of President Islam Karimov, a communist apparatchik holdover of the old regime, which, while violently suppressing opposition, encourages corruption that permeates society, including the executive branch. Bribery will win you everything from admission to leading educational institutions to a favorable outcome of traffic cases and civil lawsuits.

#10 Equatorial Guinea

One of the world's smallest oil powers, it is also among the most corrupt. Still, possibly under pressure from the major oil companies that operate there, particularly Exxon Mobil, things have improved a trifle, though the corrupt President Teodoro Obiang Nguema remains in power. Now, though, it's becoming possible to operate a business on a reasonable basis, provided one accepts that 30 percent of all funds, including oil profits, go straight into the pocket of Nguema. Still, the system of corruption now is more rational and orderly than the previous system that amounted to near-total anarchy. (Andelman, 2007).

In addition to corruption, there has been a history of U.N. waste and program mismanagement. All you need to do is a Google search and a very long list will appear containing a wide range of stories and examples. We call them "diplomats," but in my opinion, they are a community of do-nothing politicians. While people are starving to death and cultures are being ravaged by sickness and disease, some U.N. diplomats are attending gala receptions, drinking champagne, and eating caviar. They are drunk with the arrogance of power. Their egos and self-centeredness fuel their desire for individual gain at the expense of the poorest of the poor around the world. They sit back comfortably, secure in their inner world of greed and power, while people in the world are being murdered, starved, and abused by corrupt governments. There is no quick and purposeful intervention on their part to right these wrongs and address these transgressions against humanity. They talk and debate and then talk more and debate more, which perpetuates a cycle of inaction, when they should be taking swift and deliberate action.

There needs to be a new world order that recognizes the unique diversity and cultural norms of a global population, while at the same time establishing some universal standards of humanity. To sit back and do nothing when corrupt political leaders and their governments are brutalizing, murdering, and raping citizens is absolutely wrong and should require immediate intervention on the part of the United Nations. I have included one article to substantiate my points about waste and mismanagement at the United Nations. The article was in the *Washington Post* on February 10, 2008, and was written by Colum Lynch.

Audit of U.N.'s Sudan Mission Finds Tens of Millions in Waste

By Colum Lynch
Washington Post Staff Writer
Sunday, February 10, 2008

UNITED NATIONS—The United Nations has wasted tens of millions of dollars in its peacekeeping operations in Sudan over the past three years, according to the findings of U.N. auditors examining the financial practices of the global body's overseas missions.

U.N. officers in Sudan have squandered millions by renting warehouses that were never used, booking blocks of hotel rooms that were never filled, and losing thousands of food rations to theft and spoilage, according to several internal audits by the U.N. Office for International Oversight Services. One U.N. purchasing agent has been accused of steering a $589,000 contract for airport runway lights to a company that helped his wife obtain a student visa, while two senior procurement officials from the United States and New Zealand have been charged by a U.N. panel with misconduct for not complying with rules designed to prevent corruption.

The U.N. procurement division "did not have the necessary capacity and expertise to handle the large magnitude of procurement actions" in Sudan, particularly during the early phases of the mission, according to a confidential October 2006 audit obtained by *The Washington Post*. Investigators also detected "a number of potential fraud indicators and cases of mismanagement and waste." (Lynch, 2008)

Here is what I recommend our government do to correct this ineffective, worthless, and elitist organization. First, we need to demand that the United Nations reform itself. It should be expected to recreate its organizational charter. Given the global nature of the problems the world is facing today, the United Nations needs to reengineer how it is structured. This restructuring should include all agencies, departments, and programs—those that do not add any real value to the world at large need to be eliminated. It also needs to de-layer the bureaucracy by eliminating levels of management and bureaucrats. The goal should be to streamline all departments, programs, and agencies so as to be able to respond quickly with the necessary resources to deal with humanitarian crises anywhere in the world. In addition, it needs to step in quickly and respond to political situations between countries that could lead to armed conflict. It needs to be very decisive in dealing with issues such as terrorism, genocide, sex slavery of children and women, and armed aggressions. It needs to become an active force in dealing with the global environmental problems such as pollution, population growth, and resource depletion. No country would be excused from U.N. scrutiny when it comes to pollution and resource depletion. This means no waivers should be given to countries like China, Russia, Africa, or India.

Since the United States contributes more money than any other country to the operating budget of the United Nations, we should mandate these reforms. We should tell the United Nations that unless major reforms start to take place throughout the organization, we will reduce our contribution by 20 percent per year. If nothing of significance in the way of major reforms happens during a five-year period, we will withdraw from the U.N. and contribute no more money. If this happens, we should create a new world organization.

We also should demand that the European Union step up to the plate and actively engage in the resolution of many world conflicts. The European Union, as well as Russia, China, and Japan, need to take a greater leadership position in resolving global problems. The United States should become more of a partner in the process of addressing the world's problems and less of a cop. We are not the policeman of the world and should not try to bully other countries.

Democracy may not be for everyone and every culture. Personally, I do not care if Cuba is a communist country. Who said our model of government should be the only one that all countries must adopt for their way of governing? Yes, human rights are important, but there are issues that the world community must deal with and resolve first and foremost. We should not impose our standards on other countries, cajole or bully them to agree with our human rights political agenda, or have our senior government officials embarrass their leaders in public. When people are enslaved in a tyrannical system of government; when women suffer abuse, humiliation, and torture; when children are enslaved and exploited—this is when the world community needs to get involved—not just the United States.

We should continue to be the compassionate and caring nation we have always been. We should continue to assist the less fortunate nations with food, medicine, and technologies that will help them build strong and prosperous countries. However, we should not get involved in military interventions without a coalition of the other key nations of the world. Nor should we continue to give foreign aid to countries that hate us and conspire to harm our citizens or our allies. We should suspend all foreign aid, except for humanitarian needs, for a period of two years and reassess which countries we give it to, how much they receive, and how our taxpayer dollars will be spent in those countries. No more blanket cash payments to corrupt dictators or their regimes. If a country receives foreign aid from the United States, we should know how that money was spent and hold the receiving nation accountable. If a country mismanages or misallocates the aid it has received, it should be prevented from receiving any future aid from the United States.

There should be a quid pro quo with all nations which will receive foreign aid after the two-year moratorium. We should only give aid to countries that show real commitment to human rights and demonstrate a high level of respect for their citizens' welfare. We should under no circumstances give money to tyrannical leaders or those of countries that show little regard for the welfare of their citizens.

As much as we espouse the importance of diversity, we should respect other countries' rights to create a government they choose. We should not try to force-feed democracy to other cultures or societies. There is more than one way to govern a country and create a great society. We should not be interfering in the affairs of other nations unless there are crimes against humanity perpetrated against citizens—and in these cases, the interventions should come from the world community, not just the United States.

With all this being said, I ascribe to President Theodore Roosevelt's philosophy of walking softly but carrying a big stick. As I have advocated closing 50 percent of our military bases overseas, I am also a staunch supporter of maintaining a strong military. We could help our unemployment levels by closing military bases in Europe and reestablishing those base operations in the United States. We should always be prepared and never put ourselves at risk by thinking no other country would want to cause us harm. One only needs to look at China and the tremendous buildup of its military, which includes both ground and naval forces. It has hacked into our computer systems and launched cyber-attacks on our infrastructure. There are several countries in the world that are quite capable of starting a global conflict and we must be prepared. Russia is currently flying its long-range strategic bombers armed with nuclear weapons toward the United States on a daily basis, just like it did during the Cold War.

Russia to revive long-range bomber patrols

Move to show Moscow's military power amid chilled U.S. relations

MOSCOW—President Vladimir Putin said Friday that he had ordered the military to resume regular long-range flights of strategic bombers, a show of Russia's resurgent military power, which comes amid a chill in relations with the United States.

Speaking after Russian and Chinese forces completed major war games exercises for the first time on Russian turf, Putin said a halt in long-range bombers' flights after the Soviet collapse had affected Russia's security as other nations had continued such missions—an oblique reference to the United States. "I have made a decision to resume regular flights of Russian strategic aviation," Putin said in televised remarks. "We proceed from the assumption that our partners will view the resumption of flights of Russia's strategic aviation with understanding." (Press, 2007)

The article went on to report:

'A new life'

The Russian-Chinese war games, which took place near the Ural Mountain city of Chelyabinsk, coincided with Russian airforce maneuvers involving strategic bombers, which ranged far over the Atlantic, Pacific and Arctic oceans. Putin said that 20 Russian bombers were involved in the exercise. "Starting today, such tours of duty would be conducted regularly and on the strategic scale," Putin said. "Our pilots have been grounded for too long, they are happy to start a new life." Soviet bombers routinely flew such missions to areas from which nuclear-tipped cruise missiles could be launched at the United States, but stopped in the post-Soviet economic meltdown. "Starting in 1992, the Russian Federation unilaterally suspended strategic aviation flights to remote areas," Putin said. "Regrettably, other nations haven't followed our example. That has created certain problems for Russia's security." (Press, 2007)This was in response to our agreement to put a missile defense system in Poland. President Obama has decided not to go through with the missile defense shield there, and recently announced that the United States will not use nuclear weapons against any nation that has abided by the Nuclear Proliferation Treaty. The White House also announced that it would use conventional forces against any country that attacks the United States or its interests, but will not retaliate with nuclear weapons if that nation has abided by the treaty.

To me, this does not make any sense. Another nation can wipe out New York City with biological or chemical weapons and we will not use nuclear weapons to retaliate. We need to maintain the best military in the world to protect ourselves from future attacks. Just look at China, Iran, North Korea, Russia, Venezuela, and many countries in the Middle East, and you can get a sense that a major conflict is just around the corner; we need to be prepared. So, even though I advocate for the United Nations to step up and deal with the crises in the world that could lead to a major global conflict, and even though I advocate a reduction in our military footprint overseas, I also advocate a strong defense and exceptional military power. We should walk through the global community softly and respectfully while we carry a big military stick.

Chapter 10

Outsourcing, Globalization, and Our Industrial Systems

You might have asked the question when you opened this book: why did he choose *Death of the American Heart* as the title? It was purposefully done to illustrate the fact that when the heart dies and ceases to pump blood and oxygen throughout the system, the entire system will cease to function and die. What we have done to this nation over the last thirty years is sinful. It is more than sinful; it represents the nail in the coffin that will result in our demise as a great society and nation.

Our once-world-class manufacturing industry languishes in a state of continuing decline. Our once-proud manufacturing employees who worked for some of the most productive plants in the world sit quietly in deep despair, in a cold and insensitive unemployment office, waiting for the opportunity to return to a good job that provides a secure future. But we know that opportunity in the manufacturing sector is gone forever.

This demise, as I have mentioned, has mostly been due to greed. Greed in our country is like the ancient Greek mythological figure Medusa. This type of greed has multiple snake tentacles. One snake consists of our corporate leaders; another consists of our union officials; a third consists of Wall Street executives; and the last snake on this evil demon is represented by the managers and employees who resist change and struggle to maintain the status quo while we are being attacked under the banner of free trade and global competition.

There is a geographic region in the United States that can be referred to as our core industrial center. Some people call this area the Rust Belt. Others refer to it as our industrial heart. Driven by the greed of our business executives, Wall Street investors, union officials, and operating managers and employees who resist change because they are in a comfort zone, about thirty years ago we put in motion a dynamic force that would ultimately lead to the decline of our manufacturing industrial base. This base was a significant economic engine which added enormous wealth to our national economy as measured by our GDP. It provided millions of good jobs and career opportunities. Today, our once-proud manufacturing economic engine has been dismantled and sent to the four corners of the earth in search of cheap labor, resulting in a further decline of our manufacturing capabilities.

During this same period, we exported millions of manufacturing, engineering, customer call center, research and development, and information technology jobs to other nations which happened to have a cheap labor pool. Sometimes these solid middle-class jobs were moved offshore to countries that used children, prisoners, and people who were enslaved. As I previously stated, we are losing skilled and semi-skilled manufacturing jobs that were, in the past, wonderful career opportunities for our middle class, especially those young men and women coming out of high school who decided not to go to college. Years ago, they could have joined a manufacturing organization and taken advantage of a career ladder on either the technical or managerial side. These young people would become highly skilled or semi-skilled employees contributing greatly to our country's gross domestic product. These new and energized employees were proud to be producing American-made products. The employees working in these manufacturing organizations paid taxes and supported the local business community through the purchase of goods and services. Our great society was thriving, our communities were prospering, and our citizens were learning and developing new skills. As a nation, we were innovating, creating new and exciting products, and developing new technologies and processes. We were sustaining the success and development of a great society.

Let's explore the groups that contributed the most to the decline in our manufacturing sector. Pressured by Wall Street investors and an absolute need to have stock prices rise, corporate executives started to look for opportunities to reduce their operating expenses and maintain or increase dividends to shareholders. Consequently, we developed a short-term operating focus. Financial indicators were put under the microscope on a quarter-to-quarter basis. If earnings dropped from one quarter to the next, swift and decisive action was taken, in most cases without a solid understanding of the long-term consequences. Many of those actions involved downsizing and laying off employees. There was not a lot of shared ownership between different operating divisions or functions. One particular high-tech company in the Boston area, for example, had a reputation of dramatic layoffs in its divisions. It was not completely out of the question for this company to be laying off employees on a Friday afternoon in one division while advertising career opportunities in another division a few miles away in Sunday's *Boston Globe*. Any substantial down tick in the high-tech markets, such as semiconductor and computer manufacturing, would trigger massive layoffs.

During the 1970s, many companies went to Puerto Rico or Ireland to build state-of-the-art manufacturing plants so they could take advantage of a twenty-year tax exemption. This strategy on the part of corporations started the wave of downsizing and layoffs, but at the time it was only a ripple. As companies expanded, they needed to reduce operating costs and started the migration of operations to Southern states; this was not a bad strategy because the jobs stayed in the United States. However, when the flow of manufacturing jobs crossed the border into Mexico, we started to see substantial job loss. Those early job loss ripples became waves. The impact was still not that severe, but greed kept the fires stoked: greed for bonuses, multimillion-dollar salaries, and to maximize investments all led to the demise of the American manufacturing employee.

You cannot put all the blame on business leaders for the significant decline in manufacturing sectors, however. Union leadership, combined with some recalcitrant union members, has refused to allow the installation of innovative manufacturing practices on the factory floor. One small example is Ford Motor Company's new plant in Brazil. I have included a few lines from different sections of an article written by Bryce G. Hoffman of *The Detroit News*, which should give you a feel for the emotions surrounding the issue of process reengineering, and the paradigm shifts that need to take place in the thinking of our business executives, union leaders, and government officials.

FORD'S TEST BED: Brazil's Camaçari plant is model for the future

Bryce G. Hoffman / The Detroit News

At Ford Motor Co.'s factory here, a group of Visteon Corp. workers connect the wiring in a dashboard module for a Ford EcoSport. Next to them, Lear Corp. employees are building seats for the same vehicle. A few feet away, Ford's Diede Silva dos Santos applies trim to a Fiesta subcompact. She's mastered seven jobs at the plant and is working on an eighth. "If you do different jobs, it's more interesting," said Silva dos Santos, 24. "It gives me a chance to expand my knowledge. [It] makes me a more valuable employee, too, so that I will have a future here." All of them exemplify a different kind of worker in a different kind of plant for a Detroit automaker. A different way of making cars. At Camaçari, more than two dozen suppliers operate right inside the Ford complex, in many cases producing components alongside Ford's main production line. Having those supplier operations on-site allows Ford to take the concept of just-in-time manufacturing to a whole new level. Inventories are kept to a bare minimum, or dispensed with entirely. Components such as dashboard assemblies flow directly into the main Ford assembly line at the precise point and time they are needed. Unlike many U.S. auto plants, where workers' responsibilities are strictly limited to specific job classifications, workers like Silva dos Santos are encouraged to learn as many different skills as possible. Everyone—from senior managers, designers and engineers to rank-and-file line workers and maintenance staff—wears the same uniform here. The only difference is that those working for suppliers have their own corporation's insignia embroidered on their chest instead of Ford's blue oval. To appease the union, Ford painted yellow lines on the factory floor to demarcate each company's area and separate Ford's assembly operations from those of its suppliers. As in the United States, assembly workers make more than those employed by suppliers and the union is eager to ensure that work reserved for the higher-paid Ford employees is not being done by lower-wage supplier staff. Labor expert Harley Shaiken of the University of California, Berkeley, said similar concerns are one reason why the Camaçari model is unlikely to be duplicated in the United States. He said the UAW has relaxed work rules at many Ford factories to allow workers to do more than one job, and has even allowed experiments with limited supplier integration. But he said the UAW is concerned that giving too much on these fronts will just allow the companies to speed up production and transfer more and more work to lower-paid supplier employees.

"Clearly, what is going on in Brazil is pushing that envelope," he said. "I would never say never, but it would be a hard sell." (Hoffman, 2007) Granted, the use of process reengineering, automation, and robots would have, in effect, a downsizing impact on the workforce; however, it also would have made us a lot more competitive much sooner, and would have allowed our plants to retool and redesign processes to substantially reduce cost. However, as stated in the article, Brazil's Camaçari auto plant has created a total of fifty thousand jobs in the region, if you count all the suppliers, vendors, and support services that provide goods and services not only to the plant and the employees, but the surrounding communities, stores, and small mom-and-pop businesses. If our business leaders and government officials were more committed to keeping jobs in the United States, and if our union leaders, union members, and nonunion employees were more flexible regarding operational changes, job flexibility, wage and salary concessions, and work rules and procedures changes, we would not be experiencing a 10 percent unemployment rate or one of the highest home foreclosure rates in the history of our nation, and many cities, towns, and small communities might not be on the verge of financial collapse. The refusal of both union and nonunion employees to accept wage concessions and work procedural changes, and the blatant gorging of executives at the trough of economic compensation while asking for wage concessions from employees, opened the door to China as the manufacturing business partner of choice. Consequently, those unions and those employees that fought and resisted change found themselves downsized as a result of outsourcing. If we choose, there is absolutely no reason to outsource any of our key manufacturing or technology industries to China, Brazil, India, or any other parts of the world just for cheap labor. All it would take is a new way of thinking and behaving on the part of senior management, union leadership, and government officials.

The high-tech move to India and the relocation of call centers to third-world countries is a different story. In this situation, where companies have been enamored of the well-educated and cheap-to-hire

Indian software engineers or IT professionals, the move to outsource was on the basis of economics, specifically cheap labor. Why pay an American software engineer sixty to one hundred and fifty dollars an hour when you can pay an Indian software engineer twenty-five to thirty-five dollars per hour?

India and China are graduating significantly more engineers and scientists than the United States; however, we are graduating more lawyers than they are. We cannot sue our way to technological leadership in the world; we must invent our way toward it. We will not achieve this leadership position in the future unless we put a greater emphasis on math and science in our educational system and institute major tort reforms where there will be severe consequences for filing frivolous lawsuits.

Although the move of call centers to cheap-labor countries was done because of cost-reduction strategies and was enabled by technology, I believe our business leaders did not think inside the box. Certainly, from a purely strategic business viewpoint, it makes sense to outsource call centers to cheap-labor markets. I am not a socialist, but do we always have to select the cheapest option to maximize profits? Why not identify the top one hundred most depressed communities and cities in the United States and create enterprise zones? What our government should do is say to companies, "If you build plants and locate call centers in one of these enterprise communities, you will not have to pay taxes for thirty years on revenue generated from products and services produced within these enterprise zones. For every plant or research office you close in other countries and bring back to the United States, special tax exemptions will apply." Does this sound like too radical of an idea? Then why is Japan protecting its manufacturing base, and why are France and the EU protecting their aeronautical manufacturing bases?

If the above does not concern you, consider the ramifications of our current outsourced condition when faced with the threat of war. If we have a major war, our ability to develop the armament to fight will be significantly reduced. We are losing our highly trained and skilled manufacturing workers. We will not be able to produce the weapons and equipment necessary to fight a major conflict. Yes, we can recreate this skilled workforce, but by the time we do, the war might be over and we might not have been on the winning side.

Not concerned just yet? Then think about this: why are we out-sourcing some of the most sensitive equipment (electronics, defense, and aircraft components) to other countries? If they decide during a major conflict to withhold parts or become unable to manufacturer those parts, we are in trouble. We are also letting them know about sensitive technology that we are using in some of our sophisticated military equipment. Don't think for one moment that other countries will not gain from access to this technology. Also, many of the countries we outsource to do not have the same ethical value system as the United States (the value system we should be operating under).

To get you thinking, I have included some information on the trade deficit we have with China. When I state that we are losing the battle in the marketplace of products and services, this is one of the major contributing factors. As reported by the United States Census Bureau Foreign Trade Statistics, the United States trade deficit with China in advanced technology products during the three year period between 2007 and 2009 was $213 Billion dollars.

We are transferring technology and manufacturing capabilities to China, which is using our dollars to build a powerful military capability. This is not a good situation, especially if there is another global conflict. We are compromising our national security.

Also reported by the United States Census Bureau, Foreign Trade Division, the United States trade deficit with China during the ten year period between 2000 and 2009 was $1.75 Trillion dollars while our real unemployment rate exceeded 10%. This does not make any sense and it is not in the best interest of our national security to give away our technologies and manufacturing capabilities for cheap products and services so a few shareholders and executives can get richer while the majority of middle American's struggle financially.

With a $1.75-trillion-dollar trade deficit with China, it only makes sense for us to bring back some of the manufacturing operations and jobs that we have outsourced there. The American workers are more than capable of manufacturing these products at a reasonable cost. We will not be the low-cost producer, but if corporate leaders and Wall Street investors give American workers a chance, they will perform. Let's challenge Wal-Mart and other retail giants to stock and sell at least 50 percent of their inventory items with goods that were manufactured in the United States. Let's bring back the pride of a label or sticker on a product that reads "Made in America," which means it was made with care, with quality, and by American workers.

Lastly, when we outsource manufacturing or software development operations to third-world countries, we are actually teaching their workers how to use our technology. We educate them to be able to produce the products we need and use. After a while, they become highly competent and start to innovate more than we are, because we do not have to invest in additional plants, equipment, or infrastructure. We are concentrating on consuming those products and using those programs and services while they grow their economy and educate their workforce by producing and providing them. Our workforce searches for employment opportunities at Wal-Mart, Home Depot, Best Buy, etc., while their workforce is partnering with some of our flagship manufacturing corporations.

Try a simple test; take a piece of paper and a pen and list the number of people you know, including yourself, who have been downsized, laid off, or fired during the past ten years because of outsourcing. You might be surprised by the number. I know many people in the high-tech industry who have been laid off from different companies more than three times in less than four years. These brutal, bottom-line-driven corporations and their shareholders have disenfranchised, de-motivated, disempowered, and defecated on the American workforce, all because of greed and the quest for cheap labor.

Regarding free trade, it does not exist and never has. Most of our so-called trading partners do not play fair. The playing field is not level. There have been many examples over the years of countries protecting their own industries; on the one hand, they claim to be playing by the rules, but on the other hand, they make it very difficult for our exporting companies to do business in their countries. They create invisible barriers that make it hard for our managers to sell our products in their markets. For years, it was a problem to sell our rice in Japan. Certain countries banned our beef from their markets because of potential mad cow disease. China manipulated its currency, making it difficult for us to compete. Japan was accused of dumping its steel in U.S. markets at lower prices than our steel manufacturers while the Japanese government subsidized its steel industry. The EU and Airbus are no different regarding government support for their aircraft industry that put our aircraft manufacturers at a competitive disadvantage. There are many more examples that illustrate that the competitive playing field is not level.

Free trade is not free from obstacles that other countries place in front of our exporting companies. In fact, I believe that we are in a global war. To illustrate this competitive situation, I have listed below a comparison of war structures and elements, and free trade structure.

• Generals	* CEOs
• Headquarters Staff	* Executive Team
• Soldiers	* Employees
• Weapons	* Products and Services
• Intelligence	* Marketing
• Invasions	* Product Launch
• Territory	* Market Segments
• POWs	* Customers
• Casualties	* Bankruptcies
• Attack Plans	* Strategic Plans
• Battles	* Competition
• Politicians	* Stockholders
• Communications	* Internet
• Logistics	* Supply Chain
• Command Centers	* Offices
• Commandos	* Sales Force
• Tactical Moves	* Strategic Goals
• Allies	* Strategic Alliances
• Peace Negotiations	* Trade Associations

Now, to fight this kind of war, we need our government to demonstrate some leadership and support our exporting industries while insisting that the competitive playing field become level. If Japan is going to make it difficult for us to sell our rice and beef products, we should respond in kind to its cars and electronics. You are probably saying that this would start a trade war. The simple truth is, we are already in a trade war and don't realize it. We are losing our jobs, our industries, our technological leadership, and our ability to compete. We need to regroup as a country and put fairness into the various trade policies we have established over the years, as well as supporting our manufacturing and technology industries.

The president of China visited the White House in April 2010; prior to his visit, it was announced that President Obama would not bring up the subject of China's having manipulated its currency because we didn't want to offend him. When does it stop? When do we say to our so-called trading partners that it is time they play by the rules?

Chapter 11

Two Visions of the Future

The Future Is Ours to Create

I have never been an "either/or" thinker. I have always explored the possibilities that fall between the two extremes. However, in the case of our future as a great nation, I see only two visions. One is based on a series of negative forces that will create a downward spiral into the pit of mediocrity. The other vision is based on the power of positive forces driving us upward and forward into an ideal future state as a country.

The vision I see currently at work is based on a vortex of negativity. It continues to be created and deepened because we will not embrace a new (yet old, at the same time) set of core values as a country, based on respect, honesty, integrity, compassion, caring, hope, and personal accountability for one's behavior, actions, words, and deeds. As we, as a country, continue to purge God and religion from our society, that void will be filled by evil, disrespect, dishonesty, selfish ego-driven behavior, a lack of compassion and caring for others, and a disregard for the feelings and possessions of other American citizens. As more and more people look for a handout versus a helping hand, as they try to scam the system, as they continue to exploit their employers, neighbors, and shopkeepers, our society will crumble into a state of apathy and mediocrity. As we hurry about our daily lives, never once thinking about or helping the less fortunate, we ourselves will become lonely and isolated. As we allow the most unfortunate of our society to continue to suffer in poverty, our children to go to bed hungry, our elderly to endure the trials and tribulations of aging in places of loneliness, and our students to be denied a good education, we will have lost forever the vision of our founding fathers. If we continue to bully the world community, we ourselves will become bullied.

Imagine America as a second-rate country—certainly not a third-world country, but not an exemplary civilization. All the good that we, as a great nation, could have done to feed the poor around the world, to clothe those without clothes, to heal the sick and eliminate diseases that ravage people in developing nations will not have happened. Think of the technology that we will not have developed that could have been so beneficial to mankind. As we slip into this morass of despair and hopelessness, think of how we have let down our parents, grandparents, founding fathers, and those countless millions who gave their lives to build this great nation and those who died defending it.

Think of what we are doing to our children and theirs. We are condemning them to a life of misery and hopelessness. Future generations will not experience the great society that you and I have experienced. They will not feel the greatness of our nation nor see its good work in the world, raising the standards of quality of life for all mankind. We will lose our leadership in the league of nations and become a follower as opposed to a trailblazer. A thousand years from now, think of what people will say about the United States of America: "It did so much good in the world. It was such an advanced civilization. It had everything going for it. What happened? If only it had not collapsed. I wish I could have lived back then to experience such a great civilization." We will have become just an artifact on the archeologist's shovel.

Well, it does not have to be this way. We have a choice as a nation to create a vision that will lead to a greater dimension of success and position us to lead the world instead of follow. We can create and embrace, throughout every part of our great land, a vision of an ideal future state—a vision based on a set of values and guiding principles that allows room for God to walk side by side with us on this journey into the future.

We will once again become a nation where all citizens are compassionate and care about their fellow citizens and mankind in general. Our citizens will demonstrate respect for all individuals and their property. Personal accountability will guide behavior, and one will easily accept personal responsibility for words, actions, and deeds. We will catapult ourselves to the forefront of nations as the most educated population on the planet. We will feed and clothe the poor of the world. We will eliminate diseases that ravage people in underdeveloped nations. We will be the leader in new technologies that create the energy sources we will need in the future. We will teach and help poorer nations to grow food and educate their populations in order to raise their quality of life.

No child in America will ever go to bed hungry. No child in America will ever go without a visit from Santa Claus or a gift. The family will once again be the centerpiece of strength and guidance. No child will ever be denied the opportunity to be educated, and that means access to college or technical school. Marriage vows will mean something, and there will be a father in the lives of most children. Americans will be able to safely walk the streets anywhere in the country. Our parks and playgrounds will be safe and clean. We will have the most advanced transportation system in the world. No one will ever be denied quality health care. Our elderly will live out their remaining time on earth with dignity. We will conquer the most deadly and debilitating diseases. Our prisons will not be overcrowded with our young minority men. Instead, because of an excellent education in a modern, state-of-the-art school facility and a good job upon graduation, they will be productive members of our society.

A Summary

I recommend the adoption of the following proposed vision, set of operating principles, shared values, and aspirations for our nation.

Our National Vision

The United States of America will strive to become the most compassionate, caring, and supportive nation in the world. Our citizens will be the most educated workforce on the planet and will dedicate themselves to improving the quality of life for all mankind. We will lead the world in the development of technology. Whether it involves medicine, food, clean water, energy, science, or transportation, we will develop and deploy these technologies throughout the world.

Our National Global Operating Principles

In our dealing with other nations, we will:

- Teach and not tell
- Counsel and not criticize
- Value and not vanquish
- Support and not scold
- Respect diversity and not try to force compliance
- Lead and not manage
- Promote a hand and not a handout
- Be forthright and honest and not deceiving
- Earn respect and not demand respect
- Help and not forget
- Cure and not confuse
- Feed and not ignore
- Tolerate and not condemn
- Cherish and not control
- Love and not hate

Our National Core Shared Values

Finally, we will once again be guided on our journey to greatness by embracing and modeling the following core values:

- Respect
- Honesty
- Personal integrity and ethics
- Trusting and trustworthy behavior
- Loyalty
- Compassion and caring
- Personal accountability
- Morality

Our National Aspirations

In our future society, our vision, operating principles, and core values will allow us to:

- Educate everyone
- Feed the hungry
- Help the poor
- Cure the sick
- Eliminate crime as we know it
- Establish values throughout the land
- Be guided by morality
- Be honest in all our dealings
- Fix the systems that serve our citizens
- Provide a good job for everyone
- Raise our standard of living
- Become exceptional stewards of the environment

We will make this journey with the power of a higher spirit as our guiding light.

Chapter 12

The Final Chapter

Before you read my conclusions and recommendations, I offer a series of thought-provoking questions I'd like you to think about as you read this chapter. The questions are as follows:

1. Are you better off financially than you were ten years ago?
2. How has your 401(k) or retirement plan been performing? Have you lost money (value) or gained value over the last few years?
3. How many family members, neighbors, acquaintances, or work colleagues do you know who have been adversely affected by outsourcing, downsizing, or globalization?
4. How has the value of your home been doing lately? Has it appreciated or declined during the past eight years?
5. How is your economic situation? Have you received salary or merit increases commensurate with your performance and contributions to your organization?
6. Do you and the other working members of your family feel more secure or less secure in your jobs?
7. Are you being asked to do more work, work longer hours, and be more flexible and open to change? If so, are you being compensated for your increased level of work and commitment to the organization?
8. Do you feel that your elected officials are representing your interests more than they support special interest groups?
9. Do you feel that middle-class American citizens are being fairly supported by our government and business leaders?
10. How is the mortgage foreclosure rate in your neighbor? Is it acceptable?
11. How well are your local schools performing?

12. Is the behavior of America's citizens becoming more moral or less moral?

13. Are our citizens more caring or less caring of the disadvantaged among us, or are they preoccupied with self-interests?

14. Does the global community care about our country and the well-being of our citizens, and does it play fair and by the rules when it comes to the global competitive marketplace?

15. Is Congress more effective or less effective than it was ten years ago?

16. Do your children and grandchildren have a brighter, more secure future, and will they have the opportunities for a higher standard of living than you had at their age?

17. Will the children born during the next ten years come into this world burdened by debt that an out-of-control Congress established during its watch?

18. Ten years from now, will America still be a leader in science, technology, medicine, food production, and manufacturing?

19. Will our military still be able to defend our nation and maintain its superpower status, ensuring that the forces of evil do not jeopardize the welfare of the world?

20. Will God, our traditions, values, and beliefs continue to be diminished in their ability to influence our moral behavior and culture?

21. Finally, will America continue to be the greatest nation ever on this planet, or will it fade away into history's closet of civilizations that were once great but could not sustain their greatness? Will we survive?

I realize that I have included a lot of questions for you to think about. My hope is that they will get you to reflect upon your current situation, our country, and the future of your children—and what you might be able to do to influence or change things for the better. Now, I would like to invite you to read the final chapter.

Is there hope for our great nation? The answer is, unequivocally, yes! There are tens of millions of great Americans yearning for change. They are men, women, and children, old and young, which make up a tapestry of cultures, ethnicities, religions, and ideologies. They are what many have called the melting pot of our society. Some are new to our land, some have roots going back generations, and some have ancestral roots that go back thousands of years. They all make up the human face of America, and they embrace and live under the constitutional philosophy of **"We, the People."**

The Declaration of Independence clearly states:

We hold these truths to be self-evident, that all men are created equal, that they are endowed by their Creator with certain unalienable Rights, that among these are Life, Liberty and the pursuit of Happiness...That to secure these rights, Governments are instituted among Men, deriving their just powers from the consent of the governed...That whenever any Form of Government becomes destructive of these ends, it is the Right of the People to alter or to abolish it, and to institute new Government, laying its foundation on such principles and organizing its powers in such form, as to them shall seem most likely to affect their Safety and Happiness.

Our current government has become destructive because it is dysfunctional. Therefore, we, the people, not only have the right, but the duty, to change it.

- **We, the People,** deserve honest elected officials representing us. If it turns out that they are not living by a code of conduct that models the highest ethical standards possible, then we should vote them out of office and demand reforms that lead to integrity and accountability.
- **We, the People,** should band together in a quiet and peaceful revolution, using the power of our voices and the muscle of our votes to demand a balanced budget. No more pork. No more earmarks. No more backroom deals. No more special interest group desires over the needs of our citizens. No more personal agendas influenced by greed and dishonest behavior. We need to take back our government by the power of our united demonstrations.
- **We, the People,** need to take back our schools and start to create an educational system that will position our

kindergarten through twelfth-grade students to be able to successfully compete with the best of their global counterparts. The ultimate goal should be for our children to be the most educated in the world.

- **We, the People,** must say no to teacher unions and no to tenure for teachers who are inept. We should institute a performance-based model for all teachers and school administrative staff.
- **We, the People,** should demand reforms that lead to excellence in all our schools, no matter where they are located.
- **We, the People,** should dismantle the bureaucracy within our federal and state departments of education and create a new values-based science- and technology-driven educational system in all grade levels.
- **We, the People,** should demand that our traditions and values be honored and embraced in every classroom.
- **We, the People,** should expect that during a two- or four-year college degree program, significant emphasis is placed on ethics, integrity, and personal accountability.
- **We, the People,** should demand that, first and foremost, our business leaders think and act in the best interest of our nation. To lay off and destroy the lives of millions of American citizens so we can save a few dollars on products or make a few more dollars of profit is morally reprehensible. Given the right type of visionary leadership, we can reestablish a viable manufacturing industry in our country and once again demonstrate leadership and innovation. This requires vision and commitment on the part of our business leaders to invest in the necessary technologies, plants, and equipment that will allow us to competitively manufacture products in the United States. It requires vision and commitment on the part of our political leaders to create tax, environmental, and regulatory policies friendly to business and in alignment with how other countries are supporting their manufacturing industries. It will require vision and commitment on the part of our union leaders to be reasonable in setting work rules that don't stifle creativity, innovation, and out-of-the-box thinking, as well as pay scales that don't force companies to outsource as their only alternative to reducing cost.

I would like to take a moment to review what I consider to be some of the most significant recommendations that will help to transform our nation to a state of greatness once again. If we embrace and implement these recommendations, and if we honor the spirit of our founding fathers, our Constitution, the Bill of Rights, and our moral heritage, we will once more be the leader in the free world and keeper of the light of liberty. My overarching recommendations are as follows:

1. The president of the United States and Congress shall create a new national vision for America that will act as the engine for change and transformation, allowing our nation to once again achieve a state of greatness like the one that President Kennedy created in the '60s. Through President Kennedy's vision of putting a man on the moon, he put America in first place as the greatest nation that ever existed. The ball rests in President Obama's court to craft such a vision and have Congress approve it as the driving force and beacon of light for our nation to aspire to achieve.

2. The president of the United States and Congress should create a core set of shared national values that will permeate every corner of our society and touch every citizen. These shared values should be reflected in the behavior of all American citizens, regardless of age, profession, economic status, religion, or political affiliation. These values should be reflected in all policies and laws that are developed by our federal, state, and local governments.

3. Businesses and organizations of all types will need to embrace these shared values in their interactions with clients, customers, consumers, employees, business partners, suppliers, key stakeholders, and constituents.

4. Schools, colleges, and universities must create institutions that support, reflect, and reinforce these shared values as they go about the business of educating our children, young men and women, and future leaders of our nation. Values, ethics, and person integrity should be included in the core teaching curriculum for all grade levels.

5. We must maintain our traditions and holidays as a nation, and be tolerant and supportive of the cultural diversity and unique traditions of the various groups that represent the tapestry of our citizens.

6. We should be able to make room for the various gods our citizens worship as we pursue our national vision. There should always be room for one's god on our journey to sustained greatness as a world leader.

7. The president of the United States and Congress must develop a set of strategies that will rebuild our manufacturing base. These strategies should include the creation of a tax policy that will help attract manufacturing back to the United States and is business-friendly.

8. Enterprise manufacturing "no tax" zones should be established in the hundred most impoverished communities in the United States. Extra tax incentives should be given to any company that returns to the U.S. the production of products and the operation of services that were previously outsourced to offshore vendors.

9. The president of the United States and Congress should create a law requiring that the budget be balanced. No deficit spending should be allowed. This law should also mandate a "one item, one bill" requirement. No more pork or add-on projects should be allowed. Each appropriation should stand on its own merits.

10. There should be mandatory prison sentences for politicians, lobbyists, and business leaders doing business with the government who are convicted of corruption. These convicted individuals should serve hard time—no more country-club prisons.

11. Congress should rewrite the tax code to be a flat tax for both individuals and businesses—no more special deductions. You make X, you pay Y—no more writing off your vacation home, boat, trips, etc.

12. Utilizing the available technology, we should downsize the federal government by at least 30 percent. We should reengineer every federal agency and eliminate those that do not add value anymore, are redundant, or do not meet the means test for being critical to the core mission/purpose of the federal government. We should shift as many services as possible to Internet transactions.

13. We should immediately reengineer our kindergarten through twelfth-grade educational systems. We should start by significantly reducing the bureaucracy of the U.S. Department of Education and recharter the agency with creating the necessary protocols, policies, and actions that will position our children as the most educated in the world, with top rankings in math, science, and technology. This redesign should include the creation of a two-track system, one track being academically oriented and the other technology oriented. The technology track should include studies in green technology, bio-technology, computer technology, chemistry, physics, and science.

14. As soon as our children are toilet trained, we should start their basic educational process, which will include a foundation in reading, math, science, technology, and a foreign language.

15. The U.S. Department of Education should be downsized and the freed-up assets reallocated to the states for the purpose of creating centers of educational excellence, especially in high-crime, high-poverty, and high-dropout areas.

16. To be eligible for the reallocated funds, each state must reduce the ratio of administrative personnel to teachers. Each senior-level administrative person must teach one class per semester.

17. In addition to stimulating the minds of our children, we should also work on building physically fit and healthy students at all grade levels. Physical activity and good nutrition should be built into the curriculum at all grade levels.

18. The school day should be lengthened to match that of other nations with which we are competing in the global marketplace.

This will also allow our schools to develop intramural sports programs in which all students must participate during the school week.

19. Teachers must participate in mandatory training each year that meets specific knowledge standards and they should receive performance evaluations based on results. If they don't meet the knowledge standards and their classroom performance is below par, they should be put on a developmental plan to correct their performance. After one semester, if they have not improved their performance, they should be placed on developmental probation designed to increase their level of competence. If after two full school years their performance has not improved substantially, they should be terminated.

20. We should immediately issue a mandate for the United Nations to reform and eliminate corruption. The U.N. should be required to restructure itself to become more effective and efficient. Just like our federal government, the United Nations must conduct an agency-by-agency performance review and eliminate any agency or part thereof that is not adding value to the citizens of the world. The United States should start to reduce its contribution to the U.N. by 20 percent per year if there are no substantial signs of reform.

21. Congress should pass laws that are aimed at reforming our legal system. Strong tort reform should be mandated, with the goals of eliminating frivolous lawsuits, streamlining our judicial process, capping damages awarded, and placing accountability for one's personal actions in the process. Medical malpractice laws should be established to bring fairness and sensibility into the process, which will not adversely affect good doctors.

22. Stiff, swift, and mandatory penalties should be established to curb the Medicare and Medicaid fraud that is currently rampant in the system. Violators should be sent to jail quickly. The government needs to redirect some assets from other agencies to identify the most corrupted areas of the country, and with a SWAT-like mentality make the necessary interventions to put the cheats in jail.

23. We need to restructure how we provide foreign aid to other countries. We should place a moratorium on all financial foreign aid for a two-year period. No money should be given to any country during this time. Instead of providing money during these two years, we will continue to provide food, medicine, and technical support as needed, but financial payments should stop. During this period, we should profile the needs of our own country regarding roads, bridges, light rail, hospitals, and school upgrades, and allocate some of these earmarked foreign-aid funds to improve our own infrastructure. We will not give money to dictators and government leaders who oppress, torture, or disrespect their citizens. Instead, we will use other channels to provide food, medicine, and infrastructure support.

24. We must allow our traditions and holidays to be honored in all our facilities. We need to reverse the trend of being too politically correct and allow our children, for instance, to celebrate Christmas, Hanukkah, etc., in schools and other public places throughout our great land.

25. Congress must create a law that prohibits add-ons and pork to bills. We need a "one item, one bill" law. Congress can create other mechanisms for dealing with special projects using the conference committee and subcommittee infrastructure. Major legislation must stand on its own and not be hijacked with pork spending projects as legally attached parasites.

26. Congress and the president of the United States must maintain a balanced budget. No more deficit spending.

27. The silent majority needs to become more active and form the basis for a viable third party.

28. We are no longer at war with Germany or Japan, so why not close our foreign military bases? We could save tens of billions of dollars a year if we close 50 percent of our bases overseas. All of this money could be allocated for education and enterprise manufacturing zones. The Cold War is over and a new strategic defensive plan regarding global bases needs to be developed.

29. We must stop trying to purge God and patriotism from the lives of our children. The framers of our Constitution identified the issues with the separation of church and state, but we have gone way too far in trying to be politically correct. Bring back school prayer and have our children not only say the Pledge of Allegiance to the flag, but sing "The Star-Spangled Banner" every day. We should make it okay to talk about the heroes of our past, and to honor and respect the men and women who wear our country's uniform.

We can and we must take back our country.

The silent majority is desperately looking for both our political and business leaders to create and drive the visions that will lead to our greatness as a caring, compassionate world leader. We cannot, nor should we, leave our children in a morass of mediocrity. Be it by voice, by vote, or by the force of our passion, **we, the people,** will not let this nation travel down the path of time lacking a vision of greatness for it and all its wonderful citizens.

The time has come. The melting pot is boiling with passion for change and transformation. We can make a difference. You can personally make a difference:

- Get involved.

- Run for school committee/board.

- Vote out politicians who lack character and vote in politicians who demonstrate character and integrity.

- Don't buy products from companies that don't care about American workers.

- Say no to union greed.

- Demand reform in your schools, local government, and workplace.

- Don't settle for poor quality products or services.

- Pay a little more and shop in stores that carry a balance of merchandise that is made in America as well as overseas.

- Demand that our holidays and cultural traditions be honored in your local schools.

- Demand that teachers and administrators are held accountable for the performance of students and schools.

- Reinforce the values of family within your home.

- Establish and constantly reinforce a set of core values within your family, and in youth groups or sports teams with which you are associated in your community.

- Volunteer, and go out of your way to help others in your community who are less fortunate.

- Do something nice for someone else every day. Make sure that everyone in your family does this. Small acts of kindness do matter and will amount to something very special.

- Don't sit back.

- Don't be quiet.

- Be passionate at work and look for opportunities to create positive change.

- As you become involved, say a prayer for the sick and dying, the poor and oppressed, and the lonely and starving people of the world.

Become an agent for positive change with your voice, with your vote, with your behavior, with your passion, with your heart, and with your soul. Embrace the core values of our heritage and model those values. Demonstrate your beliefs and principles in all aspects of your personal and professional life. Expect excellence from those who serve our citizens. Believe that you can make a difference to help create a better future for the next generation of Americans. You can become a Pilgrim, helping to establish new thinking paradigms that will create the reestablishment of the cultural fabric that will make us an exceptional nation of opportunity for all American citizens who want to taste success through their hard work and personal diligence. You will be helping to rekindle the American dream for many of our people. You can become a Patriot, ensuring that our constitutional freedoms live on and that our laws remain fair and just in their application. And yes, you can become a Pioneer, helping to create a vision and charting a new course that will lead to new frontiers of thought and behavior which will act as the framework for an ideal twenty-first-century America. Yes, you can, and yes, together we can make a profound difference in our future destiny. There is no alternative road to our sustainable success as a nation. There is only one path to choose, and that path will lead us to the highway of success. It represents the beacon of light that will energize our souls and guide us on our journey. For it is your destiny to make a difference in this wonderful country of ours.

About the Author

Peter Hughes is president and chief executive officer of HPL University and High Performance Leadership, Ltd. He is the founder of the OD Think Tank, Global Leadership Institute, Service Delivery Leadership Institute, and cofounder of the High Performance Leadership Center. These organizations provide management education, organizational development, and business consulting services focusing on creating outstanding leadership and group behaviors within organizations. They also specialize in developing highly effective teams and process improvement.

Peter has consulted with a broad base of companies, industries, and institutions, including academic, pharmaceutical, medical devices, computer, software, Internet, Web design, retail, banking, traditional manufacturing, independent distribution, and government in the United States, Europe, South America, and Asia. He has designed and implemented organizational development interventions for these organizations that focused on areas such as leadership development, team building, process reengineering, new product development, customer satisfaction, total quality, management education, executive coaching, and cultural change.

Peter's education includes a master's degree in education specializing in management and organizational development from Antioch University, Cambridge, Massachusetts, with undergraduate studies at Temple University in the area of industrial management. He is a past winner of the Johnson & Johnson Company's Claude V. Swank Manufacturing Excellence Award for outstanding performance in the areas of quality, cost, and productivity. He is also the recipient of three Presidential Commendations from President Reagan's Committee on the Employment of Disabled Youth, due to his efforts in teaching disabled students job interviewing and assimilation skills, and curriculum development. He was featured in the *Handling and Shipping Management Magazine* for the results of his work in reengineering Millipore Corporation's World Wide Distribution Center.

Peter has been affiliated with Cambridge College for the past ten years as a senior faculty member, teaching graduate-level courses and seminars in management and organizational development. He also is a part-time faculty member at the University of New Hampshire's Whittemore School of Business and Economics, where he teaches organizational behavior.